Money Together

How to find fairness in your relationship and become an unstoppable financial team

HEATHER BONEPARTH

and

DOUGLAS BONEPARTH

 Harriman House

HARRIMAN HOUSE LTD
Website: harriman.house

First published in 2025 by Harriman House, an imprint of Pan Macmillan
Associated companies throughout the world
www.panmacmillan.com

Copyright © Heather Boneparth and Douglas Boneparth 2025

The rights of Heather Boneparth and Douglas Boneparth to be identified as the authors have been asserted in accordance with the Copyright, Design and Patents Act 1988.

Hardback ISBN: 978-1-80409-081-7
eBook ISBN: 978-1-80409-082-4

All rights reserved. No part of this publication may be reproduced, stored in a retrieval system, or transmitted in any form or by any means (including without limitation electronic, mechanical, photocopying, recording, or otherwise) without the prior written permission of the publisher. This book is sold subject to the condition that it shall not, by way of trade or otherwise, be lent, hired out, or otherwise circulated without the publisher's prior consent. This work is reserved from text and data mining (Article 4(3) Directive (EU) 2019/790).

Harriman House does not have any control over, or any responsibility for, any author or third-party websites (including without limitation URLs, emails and QR codes) referred to in or on this book. This book is for informational purposes only. Readers are advised to consult an appropriate professional in light of their relevant circumstances and requirements before acting on any information in this book.

No responsibility or liability for loss occasioned to any person or corporate body acting or refraining to act as a result of reading material in this book can be accepted by the publisher, by the authors, or by the employers of the authors.

This material is intended for informational/educational purposes only and should not be construed as investment advice, a solicitation, or a recommendation to buy or sell any security or investment product. Please contact your financial professional for more information specific to your situation.

01

Printed in the United States of America.

Author photograph by Sylvie Rosokoff.

Cover design by Charlotte Smith, based upon a concept by Christopher Parker.

CONTENTS

Introduction	1
Our Story	7
A Note About The Questions In This Book	13
Part I. Beginnings	**15**
1. Your Story = Your Story	19
2. The Places We Belong	25
3. You Still Have To Swim	35
4. There Is No Normal	40
5. The Family	46
6. Words We Can't Hear	55
7. The Hardest Work	60
Your Questions On Beginnings	68
Part II. Mistakes	**69**
8. The Croissant	73
9. Diablo	79
10. Mistakes Versus Missteps	85
11. The Thirstiest	91
12. Wishful Thinking	97
13. What Happens Next	104
Your Questions On Mistakes	110

Part III. Contributions — 111

- 14. WYKYK (When You Know, You Know) — 115
- 15. Caregivers Are Providers — 122
- 16. Divide And Conquer — 132
- 17. A New Recipe — 139
- 18. Full Circle — 145
- 19. Pamela — 152
- *Your Questions On Contributions* — 161

Part IV. Power — 163

- 20. Our Tiny Rebellions — 167
- 21. Two Sides, Same Coin — 175
- 22. In Between — 181
- 23. The Power Of Expectations — 188
- 24. Under The Influence — 194
- 25. The Signs — 199
- *Your Questions On Power* — 205

Part V. Risk — 207

- 26. The Ride — 211
- 27. No Ceilings — 220
- 28. Livin' On The Hedge — 227
- 29. A Million Ways Home — 233
- 30. The Greatest Risk Is Doing Nothing — 237
- *Your Questions On Risk* — 240

Resource Reminder — 241
Acknowledgments — 242
About The Authors — 246
Endnotes — 247

INTRODUCTION

A newlywed couple sat for lunch at an outdoor café tucked into the cliffs of the Amalfi Coast. They must have been in their twenties, like us.

Positano gives a postcard type of romance. Surprises live around every corner.

But do honeymooners love surprises?

It probably depends on what they are.

Over a cold seafood salad, the couple began to argue. He thought her parents were paying off her student loans. She didn't even *know* he had credit card debt. How could he not tell her? Well, truth was, she had some, too. They would pay their debts off together—no, separately; they would keep their accounts separate. They would pay their own debts and split their expenses. But she made more money—shouldn't she pay more?

Honeymooners don't love *these* types of surprises.

We focused on slurping the broth from our giant bowl of mussels to make it less weird. What a mess. See, we were there, on our own honeymoon, dining right next to them. We weren't trying to eavesdrop, but the café corralled all the young couples giving off our not-so-invisible American Tourist vibes together. We had to weather this couple's first fight over money until the bitter end, or our check came. Whichever happened first.

I remember laughing about it later that night. As if we had it all figured out.

Douglas and I often tell people that we lived the life cycle of some marriages before even getting married. We made big mistakes. Took big risks. We loved big. By the time of our wedding, ten years after we met freshman year in college, we were ready to take that victory lap around the dance floor. Our wedding felt like a curated statement; the arc of a story we already wrote the words for. But when the coiffed spectacle ends, reality's a whole lot messier.

Everyone dreams of what they think their lives will look like. You have your own beliefs and aspirations, which pre-date whenever your partner noodled his way into that dream. So does he. When you get together, those dreams don't just disappear—nor should they. You both bring them along.

How can you marry the expectations you've set for your own life with the person you love? At some point, your loose conversations have to turn concrete. Your dreams need real roadmaps. Your glossy filters and loving proclamations take a backseat to the effort it takes to make your relationship work. Words still matter, but actions matter more.

No actions are harder to harmonize than how two people approach money.

Nearly three in four married or cohabitating Americans believe money is a source of tension in their relationships.[1] If you're a living, breathing person who has ever shared anything with anyone—even a roommate—this shouldn't come as a surprise. But I think statistics like these make it too easy to assume that all disputes over money are about solving scarcity problems. In other words, couples only fight over money because they don't have enough of it.

Forbes examined the relationships of the 50 richest people in the United States and found they got divorced at pretty much the same rate as the general population.[2] Turns out, fortune and fame

INTRODUCTION

don't produce a different outcome. Couples have problems with money, whether they're naming their first used car or a university library together.

Feelings are feelings, but money's more than money. That's why having tons of it may not make a difference.

Money represents something different to everyone: trust, control, love, freedom, to name a few. Like the dreams we envision for our own lives, we start believing certain messages about money from a young age. These beliefs are molded and shaped by our own experiences and come from stories that began long before you found your partner and aren't quick to change just because you love someone. They are tethered to who we are.

For this reason, navigating your finances as a couple requires more than talking about the numbers. There are feelings behind your decisions, which impact the power dynamics in your relationship. That's why you need an approach to money that will make you both feel seen and heard.

Our goal for this book is to help you conquer money together.

As a CERTIFIED FINANCIAL PLANNER® professional and millennial money expert, Douglas often sits across the table from couples who only see the versions of their spouses they want to see. He's seen how our internalized money views do more than impact our choices—they dictate our lives, and sometimes, how we love. When clients are willing to go beyond the numbers with him, they gain more than a financial plan. They gain a deeper understanding of each other.

That's what we hope to do here.

What you'll find unique about this book is that it doesn't flow through a chronological timeline. The first book we wrote together did. Following the birth of our oldest daughter, we wrote what I could only consider in hindsight a "primer on adulting" for young millennials trying to jumpstart their adult lives. I refer to those times as *the years when big things happen*: we attend college, start our first jobs, find our first apartments, meet partners, move to big cities, get married, have babies, rescue puppies, find our people (or at least, think we do). We were in that place, too.

It's funny. The *big things* feel so hard while we're living them; and to some extent, they are. But at least navigating those *big things* comes with some degree of prescriptive advice we can latch onto. There are good ways and bad ways to manage your student loan debt. There are good ways and bad ways to finance a car.

But love doesn't abide by those rules.

Here, we take a more holistic approach. Like a scrapbook, each chapter is a snapshot of something. A period piece. A feeling. An era you lived through to share. Because when it comes to the ways that money can impact a relationship, you don't just get to be right once and be done. Despite what all the listicles and infographics might tell us, life becomes much less black and white than "surviving the wedding" or "buying the right house."

Something you never thought would mean anything to you might reveal itself as indispensable. Dealbreakers can take you by surprise or come through years of tiny cuts.

The plot of the story can change. So can you.

This book will help couples in every era of their lives approach money with greater fairness, sustainability, respect, and love.

A word on organization. Though each chapter is a snapshot, we organize them under five themes:

First, **Beginnings**: about our families, belief systems, and what informs us from the past.

Then, **Mistakes**: about the things we wish were different.

Third, **Contributions**: about the value and costs of caring for those we love.

Fourth, **Power**: about resources, expectations, and opportunities.

Finally, **Risk**: about our "what ifs" now and in the future.

INTRODUCTION

At the end of each part, we'll give you questions to prompt a meaningful money conversation between you and your partner. Move through the questions as you're reading, or sit with them until you're ready. You can use the QR code on page 14 to gain access to them on your mobile device. This way, you can have them at a time and place that's most comfortable for you both. No one even needs to know but you.

We've interviewed some of the best experts on love and money, and you'll hear from them throughout the book. Couples therapists, behavioral psychologists, financial advisors and educators, lawyers, authors, performance coaches, and more, all add important context to the issues we'll examine. Money is technical *and* psychological. Love is emotional *and* complicated. Our experts help us approach from every angle, and we are thankful for the depth their insights provide.

Remember when tabloids would feature celebrities hauling groceries or pumping gas under headlines like, "Celebs: They're Just Like Us?" We all knew they weren't just like us. But for a moment, we shared some sliver of the human experience, and that felt good. In the same vein, we will share with you real stories told to us by real couples. These snapshots of reality are as sensitive, icky, complex, and validating as you'd imagine them to be.

You might not be a first-generation American or the spouse of a former pro athlete. You might never have been homeless or felt like one more load of laundry might fucking destroy you. Your grandpa may never have sold a cardboard box factory for $100 million. You might never have told your husband you are a lesbian after meeting the love of your life under the stars. All the while, you will see slivers of yourself in these real stories no matter how different your circumstances are. We all believe in something. We all have fears. We've all made mistakes. We all dream. You're allowed to see just a piece of yourselves in other people and use that to improve your lives.

Perhaps we were naïve to presume that more couples—*any* couple! Why not?—would be willing to speak with us. But many hesitated, we realized, for good cause. Marital conflicts over money are longer, recurrent, and more consequential than fights over surface-level issues.[3] As these conflicts metastasize and impact the underlying health of a relationship, you will notice an emerging theme that it's *never* just about the money. Our conversations were as intimate as they get. Therefore, many couples we spoke with wished to have their names changed, and we respected their choices by doing so. Nevertheless, we are most grateful for all the couples who shared their personal stories with us. There would be no book without them.

Throughout these stories, you will learn about people's *whys*. They are the reasons you embody certain beliefs and make certain decisions about money. Our goal is to give these *whys* a microphone. When you read them in these pages, or hear them from your partner, you can honor them. You can respect them. You can get somewhere closer to fair.

In practice, Douglas tries not to make decisions for his clients. He'd rather lead them to choices they can make for themselves.

Same thing here. The path matters as much as the financial decisions you make. We want you both feeling good about how you get there.

So, let's go there.

We'll go first.

OUR STORY

The Boneparths aren't immune to the issues couples face around money. You will learn a lot about us in the coming pages, but I'll paint with broad strokes to get us started. Keep an eye out below for how the five parts of this book play into our story. You might even start to think about how they appear in yours.

Douglas and I are opposites in many ways. Our blood types call him a universal donor and me a universal receiver. How apropos? The astrologers caution that Scorpios and Leos are water and fire. Despite both of our passionate egos, our means of reaching our goals are quite different. Some say, this makes us a terrible match. Others say, this makes us whole.

I am an only child and grandchild on both sides of my family—a miracle baby with all the attention. But my parents divorced when I was 13, making me the main conduit between two feuding adults during the formative years of my life. Money was never something I had to think about until it became everything I had to think about. My **Beginnings** changed overnight. I developed trust issues that left me craving money. As a result, I pursued what I thought would be a high-earning career as an attorney to stamp my badge of approval in front of everyone who might have pitied or judged me in tougher times. I wanted my parents to be proud, but I think I wanted to stop needing them even more.

When you do things for the wrong reasons, they don't usually work out the way you want them to. To attend law school in the most expensive city in the country, I borrowed more than $200,000 in student loans. Then, the Great Recession hit. When I graduated in 2010, people said I was lucky to have any job, despite being woefully overworked and underpaid. I realized I made a huge **Mistake**. You'll read more about that later, but just know for now that I sunk pretty low. Without Douglas there to replace my shame with a constructive path forward, I'm not sure what would have happened.

Now, I'm 40 years old, and I cringe at the thought of needing to be saved. More on that later, too.

Douglas is the son and grandson of serial entrepreneurs. Through them, he developed an appetite for **Risk** that motivated him to always bet on himself. His parents were married for 36 years and gave him, ostensibly, a normal childhood. He is grateful for the years his dad dedicated to teaching him the fundamentals of financial planning and pushing him to become one of the youngest CFP® professionals in the country at the time. But their struggles in working together revealed deeper struggles within his nuclear family. When he quit his dad's financial planning firm and moved to New York City to be closer to me, those struggles boiled over. His parents divorced later in life, right after our first daughter was born.

We're two people—opposites—who reached the same place in different ways.

Wild, isn't it?

Our parents' divorces definitely play a role in our marriage. We would be lying to say otherwise. Like returning to sports after an injury, we are mindful of each other in ways you might not be unless you've experienced that pain. We have both felt alone in this world. We both sought a new family in each other.

I think this is the reason we never struggled to view our goals as collective when we were younger. **Power** belonged to both of us. We operated as a team, without ego or keeping score. I found a career in corporate insurance that felt much more sustainable from a work-life standpoint and was stable enough for Douglas to take risks establishing himself in the industry. I jokingly called him "the face of the relationship" and helped him grow from behind the scenes.

He always gave me credit—you can ask anyone who knew us then. But at some point, credit starts to feel like lip service. It just wasn't enough for me.

We wrote our first book together on my maternity leave after the birth of our oldest daughter, Hazel. Working on that project with Douglas was a welcomed distraction from my seismic existential fears around how motherhood would change me. (Motherhood did change me, for the better, but tell that to a first-time mom who only knew how to value her time through work.) Perhaps bigger than the lessons I learned about writing and letting go of perfection as a working mother, that was the first time I'd ever explored my toxic relationship with money.

Where did my screwed-up values come from? And why did I let them impact every single financial decision I made?

Publishing that book in my early years of motherhood also confirmed my goals: I couldn't spend my entire career climbing the corporate ladder in the insurance industry. Titles and paychecks couldn't be the only measuring sticks of my ambition. Perhaps like my blood type, I've always been a universal receiver of people's stories—stories like the ones you will read here—for a reason. Even as I achieved an objective level of success in my own profession, I began having a harder time watching Douglas thrive doing something he loves.

You could call it jealousy, but most women know it's bigger than that.

When the pandemic struck, our daughters were four and one.

Little Ruby was just starting to cruise, pulling down furniture with each waddle across the floor. Hazel's preschool closed, only to reopen months later to a fluid list of protocols and series of quarantines and patchwork of childcare drama that plagued us for years. I worked full-time from home while operating our Cruise Ship to Nowhere, each physical and mental obligation placing a heavier burden on my shoulders. My **Contributions** became something totally different.

Douglas didn't create this problem, but he was earning *three times* my salary. Our choice in whose time and career to prioritize didn't feel like a choice at all.

I grew resentful of our situation. I couldn't help it. Douglas was living his dream while I shouldered his corporate safety net, along with the invisible load that too many mothers carry alone. The pendulum had swung so far in his favor right under our noses, even as two loving partners who always paid attention. Something had to change. Our relationship depended on it.

In the fall of 2022, we leapt. I joined Douglas as the director of business and legal affairs at the firm full-time, formalizing a partnership we've always known to exist. That move paved the way for this book.

For sure, that was not our final challenge. (Working together presents tons of those!) But we've never been this honest in our feelings around money. We've never been this synergized with our goals. We've never had this level of respect for the contributions we each make to our family. And we've never been this confident we can face the future together.

See, our hope isn't just to help you solve money problems in absolute terms. When people change over time, how can you ever consider your work done? Instead, we want to help you uncover and validate feelings. We want you to find the courage to address uncomfortable pain points in your relationship. And through the process, we want you to see each other.

OUR STORY

We celebrated our tenth wedding anniversary around the time we started writing this book. Over my morning cup of coffee that day, I pieced together a Reel from photos of our life together without much forethought into its significance here. I asked, in the silly rhetorical way you speak to the internet, what was the secret to ten happy years of marriage? Then, of course, I answered.

I wrote, "You make room."

Room for each other's personalities, quirks, ambitions, and struggles.

If you can't, ask yourself why?

And when you think you've made enough room, make more.

In agreeing we could write this book from my perspective, Douglas made room for me.

A NOTE ABOUT THE QUESTIONS IN THIS BOOK

At the end of each section, you'll find questions about love and money that pertain to the theme we just discussed. They aren't all easy to answer, but that's kind of the point. Important stuff like this takes patience, care, and a bit of bravery, too.

You can ask your partner for their answers, interview style, but that won't work for everyone. Communicating about this stuff is hard, especially with one of you cosplaying as Oprah Winfrey. Many couples seek therapy for the sole purpose of communicating better. You might not be there yet, and that's okay.

You can also ask yourself these questions. Save your answers in a notebook or a notes app on your phone and share them with your partner at a stress-free, distraction-free time 20 years from now. Okay, don't wait that long, but it is very important to find the right time and environment to talk. You probably don't want to squeeze these important conversations between two mega-blocks of meetings on your WFH day; or scream them over your kids' bathtime; or muscle through them in bed when you're only half conscious.

Douglas and I talk about money in a few different settings: we take walks together in our neighborhood; we hire babysitters and plan dinners somewhere quiet with great cocktails; or if we want to be in front of laptops, we schedule actual meetings on Fridays, our slowest day of the week.

Figure out when and where will make you both the most comfortable, and dare I say, excited, to learn more about each other. Remember, if you scan the QR code below you can bring these questions anywhere you go.

PART I.
BEGINNINGS

You both know the facts. But do you know the stories?

When you're looking at your finances, the numbers need context. One couple's $20,000 in the bank might be the start of a new life. Another's might be the college fund that never quite hit the mark. Numbers in accounts don't tell stories. You do.

Our goal in *Money Together* is to help you have meaningful conversations about money. There's a lot to examine when you peel back the onion: communication styles, emotions, invisible burdens, timely problems facing real couples who are sick of being told to just stop buying cold brews if they want a roof over their heads. Decisions are much more personal than the money we use to make them. And both of your voices matter. They have to matter at home if you want them to matter anywhere else.

But before we can get you both to the table, we need to set the table.

Most of you lived lots of life before meeting each other. There were things you were taught. Things you observed. Things you inherited. Things you experienced that you'd rather forget. To navigate where you're going as a couple, you have to know where you've been. That history informs the person you are today. Maybe it'll shed light on the partner you want to be tomorrow.

In Part One, you will read about how our backgrounds influence our money beliefs and behaviors. But you'll also read about legacy, trauma, and what makes us tick. The challenge here is self-work as much as a couple's work. You might read something that is *so* your partner, or say to yourself, *damn, that's me*. There will be tools, but these first seven chapters are more about becoming curious and understanding each other. When you reach the questions at the end, you'll be ready to go beyond the facts. You'll be ready to share and receive your actual stories about money.

1. YOUR STORY = YOUR STORY

Your past is your past.
So is theirs.

Babies are funny. Between four and six months old, they start sticking their little Tic-Tac toes in their mouths. One of our daughters got her whole foot up in there once, which was impressive but beside the point. Child development experts believe this is one way for babies to "find their feet" and start becoming conscious of their bodies. Before then, they might not even know. Their awareness has to expand to even comprehend it.

"Welcome to the world," we say to them, but what a silly thing to say. We all start with our feet, our hands, our parent's faces. The world finds us all at different times.

When interviewing couples for this book, we asked people to tell us about their earliest money memory. Some had distinct stories to share, like Christopher, who worked at his papaw's doughnut shop in the Mississippi Delta. But many others never thought about it before. So, we broadened the question:

When did you first become aware of money, and how did it make you feel?

Their answers followed, and they said a lot.

People who grew up facing financial insecurity had the earliest concepts of money, for obvious reasons. Not having basic means would be hard for any kid to ignore. But even in stable enough living conditions, people still remembered their financial stress: eating meager dinners, wearing only hand-me-downs from the neighbor's kids, being told no most of the time. I'm sure at some point they asked their parents why, because kids ask why without any thought of their parents' hearts. In response, they received some version of the truth.

Their money problems required family-wide solutions. Some people we spoke with were expected to help provide for their entire families as soon as they were old enough to work. I'm not talking about "fun summer jobs at the public pool," but actual hard work. Whatever-it-took work. They grew into a responsibility to help provide for their mothers, fathers, brothers, and sisters.

It's normal to want to fix things. It's normal to think you can fix people.

I spoke with Dr. Joy Lere, a licensed clinical psychologist, about children who feel they need to act like parents. She explained that in times of need, children tend to slip into this role, but they're not really in a place to solve the family's problems. She continued, "When we take ownership over something that is outside of our control, that creates anxiety." It's a hard feeling to let go of. Many just carry it on.

Some let it drive them to a better life.

For example, Charles grew up the second of four children, his father in and out of work. Despite sometimes not knowing how their bills would get paid, they opened their small home to other family members in need. Charles was never resentful. He had compassion for others in worse circumstances than his, which shone through when we spoke. But it's clear that his background made him crave stability as an adult. He became a mechanical engineer for a major public utility, because "people always need power in their house." I could feel that as a husband and a father, he needs to be that rock.

Weathering instability as a kid teaches you things. Farmers' children know this well. Carson's family was great at utilizing what they had, but working a cattle ranch in Montana, they lived at the mercy of the seasons. Rain meant growth and drought meant, well, drought. Even war overseas could impact the price of oil for their equipment. Modeling his parents, Carson learned how to plan for the bad times in good ones. He still respects his resources and values that his wife, Kristie, does too.

Perhaps some people never forget how to live off what they have. But you didn't need to struggle financially to feel the impact of your conditions growing up.

Dr. Charles Eckhart is a licensed clinical psychologist who consults with high- and ultra-high-net-worth families, concentrating on generational wealth matters. He introduced me to Attachment Theory, which blew my mind as someone who needs therapy more than I'm equipped to lecture about it. But I'll give it a shot.

We develop securely attached or insecurely attached patterns *as babies*, based on the early relationships we form with our caregivers. Safe and consistent relationships produce individuals who can navigate the world (and their money) with trust and ease—or at least, without drama. But volatile, withheld, or inconsistent early relationships can lead to insecure attachment styles. These vary, but for our purposes, they have a profound impact on our adult relationships with our partners, children, and even money and those who manage it.[4]

Our relationships—not just wealth—define who we become.

It makes sense when you think about it. Like how babies only see as far as their bodies, we only knew the world we knew. Your perception—and the way it made you feel—formed some of your first beliefs about money.[5] This is why psychology matters as we explore our origins: you need to be able to look in the mirror and process your own story before you can effectively share it with anyone else.

"We are so influenced by our lived experience and what we learn with our first family," Dr. Lere explained. "The table is really set in terms of our attitudes, core beliefs, and unspoken rules about money. Our surroundings are what we believe money is, and then we carry that forward."

Your story is your story.

Which brings me back to our first question. Most people we spoke with grew into their understanding of money by comparison. In other words, they didn't know what they had (or didn't have) until someone else showed them. Perception colors so much of what we remember from being young. I still chuckle about our chat with Jon, an unassuming ex-trader who revealed he comes from multigenerational Manhattan wealth. I tried my hardest to press him about when he first became aware of his affluence. But he just smiled and reminded me that it was all relative. He may have lived in a fancy brownstone, but attending an elite private school on the Upper East Side, he knew kids that owned the whole block.

See, you can't only lend credence to the people whose stories are sad in your eyes. Real life isn't a montage of who had it the shittiest, nor should it be a race to the bottom for sympathy's sake. In a relationship, you cannot judge, compare, or invalidate your partner's past based solely on how you perceive it. You are not the arbiter of what was good and what was not.

Whether you were rich, poor, or somewhere in between doesn't matter. However you felt, you felt.

Douglas's childhood touches right on this point. He grew up in Boca Raton, Florida, an affluent city rife with gated communities and golf courses and luxury cars. Appearances matter there; I'd

1. YOUR STORY = YOUR STORY

argue, appearances matter more than what's real. But when it came to "keeping up," his parents weren't too interested. They drove the same 1985 Volvo station wagon for almost *20 years,* causing teen Douglas to sink into his seat at every intersection. You might be thinking, *champagne problems,* but there was more going on.

Douglas worried a lot about what people thought of him. Today, they'd call it social anxiety, but millennials just knew it as not feeling well and having no one to talk to. I was there when he got his first car: a black Subaru WRX with a two-foot spoiler and an exhaust so loud you could hear it rumbling a mile away. He spent hours detailing every inch of the car by hand, squeegeeing off the water streaks, paying cash to pop out each little dent. He said it was a matter of self-respect. I didn't get it then, but I do now.

The car mattered to him for reasons that weren't mine—reasons, as a partner, you can't diminish.

I received a car for my 17th birthday. My dad drove into New Jersey from Philadelphia to take me to the used car dealership, where salespeople showered us with tropes like "I hope Daddy brought his checkbook!" That was what people saw of us. We found my 1999 Nissan Altima I would later rename "Thomas The Engine That Can't." (At the time, he totally could.)

The day should have been a celebration, but my mom and I predictably began fighting over the car within hours of me driving it home. I won't share what she said—we are past it now—but the words were words that steal away moments. I lost a lot of good moments. My parents separated months after I turned 13, leaving an only child who just crossed the metaphoric threshold into adulthood with the actual duty of becoming an adult.

After their divorce, money became the center of everything. My mom painted a picture of scarcity; of us never having enough. I was expected to ask my dad for whatever I needed, but I only saw him for dinner on some Wednesday nights. We squeezed our whole lives into those two-hour meals. This was how money commingled with love to the point I could no longer see the difference. Questions lurked behind every question: "Do you still love me? How much?"

It wasn't about the money for me. Not even then.

By the time "Thomas" made it down to the University of Florida, he wasn't faring well. Every time I drove faster than 60 mph, he would revolt. One day, his front headlight popped out for no apparent reason. Things were looking grim, but I didn't want to ask my dad for help. I just needed to stop *asking*.

Good thing my boyfriend knew so much about cars.

Together, Douglas and I revisited the auto shop that tried to hustle me. We used double-sided tape to stick the headlight back in place. He put Thomas back together.

I took much longer.

We were lucky to meet young; not necessarily so we could influence each other's formative years, but so we could bear witness to them. Douglas had a front-row seat to my troubled relationship with money as a young adult. He didn't receive the facts secondhand without context or meaning.

Discovering that context is key. Ashley Quamme, therapist and financial behavior specialist, explained that people tend to know the facts *about* their partners without really understanding how those facts *shaped* their partners. If you weren't there, like Douglas was with me, you wouldn't know without asking.

What should you ask? We've got you covered at the end of this section. For now, just know that you both deserve more. You need to give each other a chance to look under the hood and see all the pieces that build people into who they are.

I know it's scary. You're worried they may not understand.

To some extent, they may never understand, because they didn't grow up in your household, in your family, in your life. But that only underscores the importance of unlocking emotions that connect your pasts together.

2.
THE PLACES WE BELONG

Your culture informs what you think about money.

We all come from somewhere. My whole life, I embodied the spirit of the saying, "You can take the girl out of New Jersey, but you can't take the New Jersey out of the girl." Where I'm from, the local culture becomes you. It's a piece of who you are, no matter where you go. No matter who you love.

Of course, we don't only find our culture in fixed places. We connect with each other through shared racial backgrounds, religious beliefs, social codes, and customs.*[6] People begin to absorb their sense of cultural community from a young age.

Aja Evans, financial therapist and author of *Feel-Good Finance*,

---

* For the purpose of examining economic outcomes, Luigi Guiso and his colleagues define culture as "those customary beliefs and values that ethnic, religious, and social groups transmit fairly unchanged from generation to generation."

thinks about culture like this: there's the *macro* part, elements of which are more widely recognized and accepted. And then there's the *micro* elements that reveal themselves in the messages passed down to us.

"How did the family talk about their specific life experiences to the next generation?" she would ask someone looking to better understand their past. "And how did the next generation internalize those messages about what feels safe and what does not feel safe?"

We learned through our grandmothers' cooking and our parents' stories and the way we lived amongst our neighbors and friends. These aren't just memories to reminisce over and seek comfort in. They're the foundation for how we develop our priorities and values.

In other words, we lean on our culture for more than a sense of belonging. The community that raised us taught us our earliest lessons about how to approach the world. They were the people we first trusted. Whether we realized it or not, we were looking to them for guidance. They were how we knew what to do.

When you find a partner outside of your own culture, you have a lot of learning to do. Probably some unlearning, too.

A *Financial Times* piece explored how financial models seem to be missing culture as a key factor in predicting human behavior. Relying on observations from the former governor of the Bank of England, the article mentions three problems with taking too narrow of an approach to understanding financial behaviors:

1. People tend to act in groups;
2. They have a tough time assessing risk, which can easily cloud their judgment; and
3. They have a broader and evolving concept of wealth that goes well beyond money.[7]

2. THE PLACES WE BELONG

When you think about it, culture plays a role in all three of those issues.

Whole books could be written about any one culture's financial messages. So, trust me, we know better than to oversimplify what gets built over generations into sweeping conclusions for this one short chapter. We don't need to, anyway. What's more important than showing you every way the human race differs is identifying how you and your partner might be influenced by your culture when it comes to money.

Let's begin with how people earn money. From a young age, many of us sought permission to earn money a certain way. We sought it explicitly from our parents and implicitly through our peers. The cultural norms we adopt give us that permission to go forth and do it ourselves.

Rafael's parents immigrated from the Dominican Republic before he was born. He learned to hustle young. At six, he joined his big brother's paper route. He flipped baseball cards. By eleven, he was waking up before school to clean up his uncle's bar from whatever debauchery ensued the night before. "I would do whatever it took to get what I wanted," whether he wanted a Super Nintendo or just an ice cream. Creativity—with a side of humility—was encouraged.

In terms of expectations, the bar was set at high school. Earn your high school diploma, his parents said. But he continued on to college and grad school to pursue his MBA, where he met Jennifer. (And Douglas, but this isn't about him!) Jennifer is a first-generation American who immigrated from Taiwan. "We were the diversity," she said of the New York suburb where her parents opened their jewelry business. Between her mother's bachelor's degree, her father's master's degree, and their "put your head down and work" mentality, pursuing higher education was a foregone conclusion for her; a point that doesn't dilute her actual ambition, but which fostered it through the environment she was raised in. We see how this plays out in their careers. They've both been successful, but Rafael expressed that the job was just a job—he'd always find a way to earn money. Jennifer was more loyal and wanted to climb.

Like Jennifer, Aravind's parents considered academics their top priority, too. They were Sri Lankan immigrants to Canada, well-educated and hyper-focused on ensuring his extracurriculars led to good grades and then to a good college. He met Mikayla at university, though her situation was quite different. As a result of her parents' divorce and mother's struggles with alcoholism, she dropped out of school. She was also White, from a rural area outside of Toronto where the culture valued marriage and family over a degree.

They spoke of the tensions this caused early in their relationship. Mikayla worried that Aravind's parents would view her as "trashy" (her words!) and uneducated, taking advantage of their generosity like she was just "the girlfriend" living in his parents' rental property. Meanwhile, Aravind felt pressure from Mikayla when he prioritized his MBA over getting married and having kids.

Cultural differences also show up in our actual money behaviors: how we spend, save, invest, and prioritize the dollars that we have.

Trust is a huge marker, at least in America. BIPOC communities have reason for their wariness to rely on major banks: systemic discrimination, redlining, and exclusionary lending practices have historically hindered their economic growth.[8]

Generational chasms like this are not easy to mend. Per the FDIC, differences in banking rates were still present between Black, Hispanic, and White households at every income level in 2023. For example, 10.6% of Black households and 9.5% of Hispanic households were unbanked, compared to just 1.9% of White households. Mistrust was the second-most cited reason.[9] Aja Evans notes that even after skeptical participants enter the

2. THE PLACES WE BELONG

banking system, they may not have the risk tolerance for even a high-yield savings account. They want to be able to access their money with no restriction.

However, as the financial system becomes more democratized and information more accessible through social media, Black Americans own more stock than ever before.[10] We're seeing in real time how the next generation acknowledges its past but embraces changes that stand to improve their lives and those for generations to come.

Culture can also influence our priorities. We laughed with Aravind and Mikayla about his parents' home, a Nineties time capsule draped in pink paints and black lacquer furniture. They just don't value spending money on things like home decor—if it's not broken, why fix it? Aravind inherited his parents' pragmatism, for better or worse. He used to be a terrible gift giver, and at one point, the couple stopped exchanging gifts altogether, which kind of sucked. Mikayla thought back to her early Christmases as a child and wanted to give their children the same feeling. Though their spending for the holidays isn't always as practical as he'd like, Aravind has loosened up over the years. Seeing the joy in their kids' faces made his own predispositions easier to compromise around.

There are just so many ways culture influences our money behaviors. Let's look at one more.

Vivi shared her incredible perspective on how she came into her money mindset. She grew up in the Guizhou province of China, a rather impoverished area in the Eighties, where even being a doctor and a journalist like her parents didn't earn them much beyond a living wage. But she was of the "one-child generation"— or as she calls it, the "spoiled generation"—of kids who always had two parents and four grandparents to give them everything they needed. Despite objectively growing up with less resources than her now-husband Matt, she was never afraid of not having money. Money was just a phone call away. Acts of generosity were displays of love. Though they both earn reliable incomes today, Vivi and Matt acknowledge how different their money behaviors are, from how they budget (she doesn't), to how they plan (she's trying), to how they spend (she's working on it!).

There's also a wide disparity in how we communicate around money. For some, it's a barrier deeper than language—it's what isn't being said.

For *The Atlantic*, Joe Pinsker explored the quandary of how Americans don't necessarily "talk" about money yet revolve around wealth. The significant wealth gap and commingling of our self-worth with our income leave people defensive and ashamed at both ends of the spectrum, which silences the discussion. And yet, Americans love to *show*: we care about what our homes, our cars, our handbags say about us. Many other cultures don't suffer from this same existential conflict. Some are just generally more open to communicating than we are. Others cannot afford to hide the ball, because they're truly counting coins to survive.[11]

People shared with us that they never learned about money as kids, because no one talked about it at home. Some cultures embody a very gendered idea of who should be managing a family's financial decisions, leaving women and children in the dark. Others never discuss money, because doing so is a *faux pas*, even behind closed doors.

Advika and Emanuel had to clear this hurdle early in their adult relationship. They came from worlds apart: India and Ethiopia. While her mother earned her Ph.D., Advika's family were "middle-class Indians," living in a one-room apartment, often exposed to the struggle to get by on the crowded streets of New Delhi. They moved once her mom began working for the United Nations, but Advika's parents were always very mindful to make sure she and her brother understood the value of money. They encouraged them to earn allowances through chores and to build mini businesses. As a family, they were open, like partners in a joint business venture.

2. THE PLACES WE BELONG

Advika likes to say her father was her first employer match: he met her, dollar-for-dollar, on any amount she saved.

In Ethiopia, Emanuel was a bit more comfortable earlier in life. His parents urged him to focus solely on his education. Food just appeared on the table. Culturally speaking, his relationship with his family was quite different from Advika's: "The parents are the parents, and the kids are the kids," he told us. "And you could be, you know, a 60, 70, 80-year-old-kid... but you were still the kid, right?"

They never spoke of money. That wasn't a kid's burden. In a broader sense, they never spoke of their emotions at all. So before even trying to reconcile their money personalities, Emanuel had to open himself up to Advika. That was new territory for him, as uncomfortable as it was.

One final point to consider is how different cultures view wealth in general. Some value it. Others reject it. The trickle-down impact of a culture's perception of money—helpful or harmful, prideful or shameful—can color anyone's financial goals.

Take Angie, whose parents painted a picture for her that she still struggles to process. Despite sensing that her parents earned a reasonable living, she was always told they had less than they really did. Her father's supposed salary of $200 per week, which he traveled from Taiwan to China to earn, couldn't have supported their modest-but-comfortable lifestyle. When they'd take vacations, they'd tell her they could only afford them because they'd made so many sacrifices. Sacrifice was the only reason they deserved to go.

That was a cultural script: who deserves what. Knowing your place.

Angie carried this narrative with her to America, where she earned her degree from Columbia University, and yet, was still scrubbing the floors of a local restaurant. She ate the leftovers off her customers' plates. That's all she thought she deserved: the impossible balance of seeking prosperity while projecting modesty. She could never be rich. She could never *feel* rich.

It's no surprise her parents loved Paul so much. He'd already had a professional epiphany that steered him away from the corporate flash of management consulting. When Paul met Angie in Taiwan, he was having the time of his life exploring, reading, discovering the world and himself. He was self-sufficient, but he was modest. In his worn t-shirt, one pair of shorts, and old shoes, Angie's parents appreciated everything in him that would be frowned upon in some suburban White communities in the United States. Paul chuckled that if his mother saw those shoes, she'd worry, "What if everyone thinks you're poor?"

But despite Paul's humble appearance, he believed in something Angie didn't. He believed the American script that we are allowed to pursue a bigger life, not just in wealth but in individual preference and purpose. This concept sometimes lives in direct contradiction with the collectivist viewpoint of many Eastern societies.[12]

We're allowed to *not* know our place. We're allowed to dream.

I also keep coming back to our couples from Hawaii, who taught us about living "aloha," a word that means more than "hello" and "goodbye." It's a moral code and a spirit to live by. Exist in the present. Value fewer material things and more nature, family, and community. See the good. Choose love.

Put me on the next plane.

But you see, there are helpful and harmful ways our culture can color our money beliefs. Some of them are so engrained in us that it's hard to separate our behavior from our identity, even when the former doesn't serve us anymore.

This is why we struggle bringing two cultures together in love.

When you challenge your partner about a financial belief that's shaped by her culture, she may hear something else. You're not questioning a credit card statement; you're questioning her grandmother's cooking or parent's stories or childhood friend's

2. THE PLACES WE BELONG

place in your life. This probably isn't true, but our defense systems work in mysterious ways. Your relationship could be the first time someone from outside her world questioned the way she does things.

It might be the first time she's had to question herself.

Reconciling who you're becoming with your sense of culture is incredibly hard, because both are so important. Aja Evans told me she finds clients who have improved their socioeconomic conditions still asking, "Am I allowed to step into this life and really enjoy it?"

You shouldn't have to choose, but it doesn't always feel that way.

So, how can you honor your roots but still grow together?

Start there: with your roots. Examine why you think the way you do about money. Where did those thoughts come from? Who taught you those lessons? What are the beliefs you hold dearest to your heart? Once again, look inward before you look out.

Then, inspect those beliefs together. Do they serve your lives today as adults?

One way to avoid passing judgment onto your partner is to speak narrowly, in the first person. You could say, "I worry that your reluctance to invest will prevent us from reaching our home goal." How different from saying, "Your family has always been afraid, and so are you."

The hardest part is to change.

Remember that you're not letting go of your identity. Evans notes that change can come slowly, and it should:

> What is most difficult for humans to do is to change behaviors that they have been doing for decades that have felt so rooted in who they are, but they know they're not working for where they are in their life right now. It doesn't mean that you're letting go of your identity. You're just

letting go of some practices that don't serve you, and that's the key part.

Finding that place to coexist might require traveling a distance from where you started.

One of you might have farther to go. That's okay.

But neither of you should start that journey before learning about where the other is coming from. This is a matter of respect that goes far deeper than money. It's so that neither of you wakes up ten years from now wondering who you even are.

Ask questions. Be curious. Learn to love her grandmother's cooking; and if you don't, at least you'll learn how the sauce got made.

3.
YOU STILL HAVE TO SWIM

No matter your faith, how you practice it matters.

S tory time.
Well, secondhand story time. I heard it from my friend Tali, who I reconnected with on Instagram after many years of double taps and sparse conversation.

It might actually be a thirdhand story. Maybe a fourth. Tales about God come to us like fabled games of telephone.

The story goes that a man was drowning. A boat came to offer him help, but he replied, "No, God will save me." Then, a helicopter came and offered help. He refused, saying again that "No, God will save me."

The man died.

When he met God, he asked him why he wasn't saved, to which God replied, "Hey, I tried! I sent you a boat, I sent you a helicopter...."

Different religions tell different versions of this story. The lesson, while nuanced for its intended audience, is universal: even those with the utmost faith still have a duty to protect themselves.

Take that as you will, because we're leaving it here, in a world of universal lessons. I know a hot potato when I see one. Douglas and I are not the people to go deep into why different faiths approach money the way they do.* Likewise, we can't offer you advice on marrying someone who practices a different religion than you. These are heavy lifts explored over time with your religious leaders, therapists, and grandmothers, who all walked into a bar... I kid.

Besides, even if we have different religious perspectives, all of us have more in common than you think. In his book *The Soul of Wealth*, Daniel Crosby outlines our shared views with beautiful care: "Ideas like compassion, kindness, justice, integrity, and nonviolence are shared by most cultures and creeds, although their expressions of these tenets come from different philosophical and scriptural texts."

Giving, Crosby wrote, is "the path to greater abundance." This is a cross-cultural truism recognized from the Bible to ancient Chinese texts and more.[13] We had recognized it, too: Catholic and Jewish couples both spoke to us about how important it is to give. How they feed communities that feed them back. They do this not to assure their philanthropy will be reciprocated in a time of need, but because it's woven into the fiber of what they believe is their purpose.

As a couple, sharing the same philosophical principles can serve as a guide—and a strong one at that. But you still may struggle over how your principles play out in the financial choices you need to make here on this earth. Incorporating your religion, faith, and

---

* But if you're into this sort of thing, I did enjoy the way Jonny Thomson summarized five major religions' takes on money in his piece for *Big Think*: "Rich and faithful? Here's what 5 major religions say about money" (March 17, 2023), www.bigthink.com.

3. YOU STILL HAVE TO SWIM

spirituality into your actual lives requires you to make peace with certain things.

No matter your faith, how you practice it matters.

Dr. Ashley LeBaron-Black and her colleagues studied 172 interviews previously conducted with people in Ireland and the United Kingdom. These interviews were originally set up to discuss the role religion played in their lives. No specific prompts were asked about money at all.

However, participants in *all but two* interviews referenced religion as something that either alleviated or exacerbated their financial stress. What's most interesting is the overlap: some of the ways that people said their religious practices *eased* their financial stress were just the flip side of how other people reported their religious practices *caused* them financial stress.[14]

Both can be true, Dr. LeBaron-Black told me, because so much depends on how you're putting your core values into practice.

Giving is a great example, because many of us do. How much should you give? *Who* do you give to? Douglas and I disagree about this often. He knows why it's important for us to give, but he doesn't feel compelled to give the way I do, which causes us to butt heads when more significant opportunities arise.

To be honest, giving might be too easy of an example. When you give, you're making abundance decisions. How people rely on their faith to navigate hard times is much more controversial.

Do you believe your faith absolves you of personal responsibility for what happens to you?

I'll be real: some people we interviewed sure made it seem that way. They don't all practice the same religion, so there's no need to point fingers. But when you are the one drowning in water, what role do you play in saving yourself?

If you couldn't tell, this topic isn't easy. The mere mention of it caused lots of folks to shift in their seats. But not Tali and her husband, Ram. As an observant Jewish couple facing a tough job market, they led with faith but followed with action.

Tali remembers the day her young husband came home and announced that after he finished nursing school, he was going to become a day trader. She threw herself onto their bed in tears.

"I didn't want a finance guy!" she told us. But they talked through their priorities: to make a certain amount of money so they could have kids and build a religious home together. His specific job mattered less than what it would afford them.

Ram did very well for a couple of years, but when algorithmic trading took over, he said, he stopped making money. They started racking up debt to cover their expenses and ended up in the welfare office. Ram was interviewing for jobs at a trading desk, but they all wanted candidates who could write code and create algos. Instead of sitting back and waiting for things to work out, he enrolled in classes to learn how to code. He worked at the local market wrapping meat for $20 an hour. He never lost faith, but he never stopped moving.

Build a bridge between faith and responsibility. "You have a responsibility to act based on what is within your control," Ram said.

Tali agreed: "God is ultimately in control and your security is ultimately in God, but God expects you to exhaust every possible way of doing something."

In other words, you still have to swim.

My friend Dr. Joy Lere, the brilliant psychologist you already heard from, is also a woman of faith. I worried she'd be so annoyed with me for fumbling around this topic with her. Religion? Money? Love? In *one* chapter?

She wasn't, though. She understood the trouble couples might have in finding their own financial agency in the real world, especially when you're being guided by religious principles you've maybe never had to apply before—let alone, with someone else.

"I think there is power in religious teachings to really set

3. YOU STILL HAVE TO SWIM

someone up to have principles and standards that help them flourish financially and have a healthy relationship with money," she explained. "But there is a lot of toxic messaging that happens and internalized beliefs that can really create suffering and strife for people financially when they adopt these ideologies without thinking about them critically."

Perhaps this is why some religious institutions have couples participate in counseling or guidance sessions prior to tying the knot: to build your bridge between principles and practice.

It pains me to write about the couples we met who haven't been able to do that. To be honest, these were conversations dominated by men acting in unilaterally selfish form: losing much of their families' money; leaning deeply onto others; expressing little remorse; citing faith in a moment that read less like a compass and more like an excuse.

It pains me to write that. But in those instances, the veil was too thin to not see through it. They are why I'm juggling hot potatoes, burning my hands.

Our ask is not for you to question your faith but to grow even more curious about it. Examine your customs in the context of your actions to turn a blinder faith you learned in childhood into something that's your own as adults.

As Dr. Lere so eloquently put, you can then "connect that sense of agency and authorship to your financial life. Regardless of how your money story starts, you get to pick up the pen and take ownership."

Amen.

4. THERE IS NO NORMAL

We don't all think the same, so we can't all work the same. Meet your partner where they are.

There are things we can control about ourselves and things we can't.

There are things we think we know about our partners, and things we have to discover.

You just read about how our upbringings impact the way we view the world, and in turn, our money. Many of the origin stories that form our identities are external like that:

we observe them;
we learn them;
they happen to us.

4. THERE IS NO NORMAL

But what happens when they're on the inside, coloring how you think, learn, and behave?

Some differences are harder for other people to account for. They are invisible until they're not. They are misunderstood until people care enough to understand them.

In the late Nineties, Australian sociologist Judy Singer coined the term "neurodiversity" to show that everyone's brains work differently. Since then, we've come to acknowledge, accommodate, and accept a wider spectrum of what may deviate from our fixed expectations of "normal." According to the Cleveland Clinic, common conditions that fall under the neurodiverse umbrella include but aren't limited to: attention-deficit hyperactivity disorder (ADHD), autism spectrum disorder (ASD), Down syndrome, dyslexia, and Tourette syndrome.

Indeed, "normal" is becoming an emptier word. That doesn't mean neurodiverse individuals don't face pressure to conform to society's way of doing things, all while processing life through their own unique lens. It can be painful, and that's where love needs to come in.

We're going to use ADHD as one illustration of neurodiversity that drives home an even larger point for us all: when it comes to our partners, we have to care enough to understand. We have to be nimble. And we have to find ways to meet them where they are.

Writing about this wasn't part of our plan until we spoke with James and his wife, Abigail, who has ADHD, a neuro-developmental syndrome impacting more than 366 million adults worldwide.[15] James is a CFP® professional who only recently realized he'd been trying to talk to Abigail about money all wrong.

Some of the financial challenges people with ADHD face include: remembering to pay bills on time; impulse spending; procrastinating around to-do list items like budgeting; and having trouble executing on big-picture concepts in financial plans.[16] These are just outward manifestations of what's going on inside.

Ellyce Fulmore, financial educator and author of *Keeping Finance Personal*, had me think about a neurotypical person's brain as having a club bouncer that protects most of the impulses from getting in. But in an ADHD brain, the bouncer sometimes walks away to smoke, letting the impulses in for free. Combining that impulsivity with a constant search for dopamine makes it hard for someone with ADHD to value long-term rewards. Money in your bank account might just feel like numbers on a screen.

You might feel some of these feels, too. But as Fulmore pointed out, neurodivergent people are living in a world that wasn't designed for them and doesn't accommodate them. "This creates an extra layer of 'shoulds,' because you're always trying to mask your behavior and habits to fit in."

Several people with ADHD told us they've been mischaracterized all their lives. People called them wild. Airheads. Unable to pay attention. They've been criticized by teachers and invalidated by parents, which for some, kickstarted a cycle of shame from a young age. With shame comes those "shoulds." They are trying their damnedest to do things "the right way." Sometimes, they do, but the weight of their "shoulds" grows heavy until they're at risk of just shutting down.

"If the task or the thing you need to do doesn't have an easy entry point and doesn't have specific steps, it can just completely paralyze you," said David DeWitt, a CFP® professional who specializes in helping clients with ADHD, and has ADHD himself. "The shame is in not acting in accordance with your values."

Trying to find common ground over money with your partner is even harder when your brains operate differently.

Now imagine not being told you were different at all.

Tyler felt the weight of his "shoulds" most of his life. Even when he tried really hard to do things, they just didn't work out. Growing up Mormon, he said, his community really valued productivity, and

4. THERE IS NO NORMAL

anytime he fell short felt like a "moral character problem." Until he learned the truth—at 38 years old.

Tyler has ADHD. His parents found out when he was seven, but Tyler didn't find out until he called his mom to tell her about *his* oldest child being diagnosed. Since then, his middle child has also been diagnosed with ADHD and autism spectrum disorder (ASD). Tyler believes he is autistic, too. "I had to go through a period of time where I had to reevaluate my whole life, because so much of it suddenly came into focus."

This all made sense to his wife, Kendall, a nurse. She was drawn to his intelligence since the beginning of their relationship, when he'd write her poems and love songs and handwritten letters. She didn't mind that he came on a bit strong. It was refreshing to be with a man who knows what he wants.

But she said, their first few years together were at times "maddening." He made most of his decisions based on how much things stressed him out, not what made the most sense. For example, they couldn't run errands that were just on the way—they had to be done in *his* order. He spent a ton of money DoorDashing fast food but was irate over the cost of their wedding bands. He couldn't wait to talk to Kendall about any "pet topics" that mattered to him, even at six in the morning. He thought she *should* care about these things. Tyler knows a lot about the finance world—he earned his MBA—and has obsessed over the markets, options trading, and cryptocurrency. But still, he was terrified of their budget and broader financial goals, so he shied away from those.

David DeWitt acknowledged that so many of his clients intellectually know what to do and can see when their behavior isn't aligning. But after all those years of pain and shame—the negative self-talk—they self-fulfill those words and give into the impulses to soothe themselves. Then, they're afraid to look at their money. They don't want to see what they've done.

Kendall thought, "I have this clearly intelligent husband who does things and reasons through things in ways that I just can't comprehend."

The diagnosis gave Tyler permission to look for answers. In working with a therapist and coach, he dispelled his recurring messages inside that shamed him over not caring enough. People with ADHD care a lot... perhaps too much. "Because it's so painful to think about these things you aren't solving, and you can't figure out how to solve them, you try to avoid them as a self-preservation mechanism."

To battle against the "shoulds" piling on him and his wife, Tyler's therapist had him consider that people do things because they have good reason to—not only because they should. He doesn't need to budget because he's *supposed* to budget. He has good reasons to budget and can explore what those are.

This led our talk to an inflection point. Tyler told me, he has to trust that his relationship is secure enough to honor Kendall's priorities, too. Now, when he wants her to pay attention to something, he must assume she's taken that into account and may still choose to do something else first, but she probably has good reason to. That has to be okay.

Trust comes in many forms. For someone denied the chance to know his authentic self, I can understand why this would be hard.

I felt a sadness coming from them. Both of them.

Kendall admitted as much. She always envisioned her family would be a certain way, but it may never be that way. Tyler's been out of work many times, as was the case when we spoke. They've had to move closer to family for help while she picks up more nursing work. He continues doing the personal work to find his way forward.

"I had to allow that person who never got to exist to die and move on," he said.

Tyler may not view neurodivergence as a superpower yet, but

4. THERE IS NO NORMAL

he has learned that he is no moral failure. "I think a lot of people mistake their thoughts for who they are."

Many of their partners do, too.

If you love someone, it's your job to help them figure out what works. You might be the first person who's ever taken the time to learn how your partner thinks after a lifetime of being misunderstood.

In advising neurodivergent couples, DeWitt breaks down big goals to the most micro-manageable steps. He creates milestone maps with incentives for stimulation and phased approaches with sub-tasks. Meetings should be frequent, and the work must be visible, so it can't be avoided. James, the other advisor I mentioned earlier, gamifies their personal finances for his wife with smaller, more specific targets so she can stay engaged.

Do not marry yourself to one way—assume less and check in more. It's going to take trial and error, and that's true with neurotypical couples, too.

Ellyce Fulmore suggests you draw from areas of success in your partner's life and apply those strategies to money. For example, if he needs to keep his vitamins on the kitchen countertop to remember to take them, maybe his bills need to be that visible, too.

You cannot be a source of your partner's "shoulds." Lean on outside resources like therapists, coaches, and financial advisors to marry solutions with the right language that can break cycles of feeling judged.

And just remember, not everything that's different needs to be fixed.

There is no perfect. There is no normal.

5.
THE FAMILY

*When you marry into money,
the privileges might come
with strings attached.*

Most of the stories here are from real couples, but I should warn you: we watch a lot of TV.

On the HBO hit series *Succession*, Shiv Roy and Tom Wambsgans' relationship showed viewers the ugliest tethers between power, love, and money. Tom, an interchangeable-yet-ambitious Midwesterner, salivated over Shiv, the youngest sibling and prospective heiress to the vast Waystar Royco dynasty—if not for love then for the love of what she afforded him. That is until, after being used, humiliated, and adulterated at the hand of her family for three seasons, he impregnated her, sold her out, and destroyed all hopes of a finale that rebuked gender norms. But they stayed together! We think.

No matter the outcome, their version of love isn't one most people would envy, despite the spoils that came with it.

The desire to "marry up" isn't fictional, of course. Throughout history and all over the world, families seek to elevate their position in society by having a child marry into a family of greater

5. THE FAMILY

wealth, class status, or both. I'd rather not think about the inherent inequities of arranged marriages, so we'll push that aside, along with the other reasons families put pressure on their children to marry rich. This isn't about that. It's about you, your partner, and the influence of family wealth.

So far, we've shown you how your roots influence your life. This chapter poses a different kind of influence your family can have over your finances. Let's be clear: having money is a good thing. A *great* thing! But there are quiet parts and loud parts of marrying into money. Let's explore as many as we can.

For starters, I want to discuss privilege, but not without the preface that this book builds on concepts. One stacks upon the other without overriding it. So, *yes*, you may have experienced pain from your perceived conditions as a child, *and* you may have privileges other people don't. Both can be true.

The material fruits of privilege are easy to see: second homes, fancy affairs, designer wares... maybe these are a bit cliché. But privilege also creates safety nets. We may not see them at first, because people process, utilize, and take advantage of them in different ways.

Take Joshua, whose grandfather was a titan of the chemical industry. Joshua didn't grow up with a silver spoon in his mouth, but when his parents inherited their "low-eight-figure" portion of this legacy, he came to understand one of the intangible values of wealth.

"I never had an existential fear around money," he told us. "I don't even think I realized there was an alternative to being safe."

Joshua didn't have to look at tuition rates for college, because he knew it would be paid for. Afterwards, he got to pursue the low-paying, entry-level jobs he wanted in politics, because earning money wasn't the priority. It didn't have to be: "I cared more about good, impressive titles than about salary, because I figured I'd get a high-paying salary someday." He could afford to take big swings knowing his safety net would catch him.

I met lots of kids like this in New York City. At the tail end of the Great Recession, almost none of my law school classmates could find a good salaried job. But some of them could afford to accept unpaid internships or stipend jobs after the bar exam. They could earn their stripes without having to pay their own exorbitant rent or repay any student loan debt from school. A decade and a half later, many of them still work in their dream industries, proving that the freedom to try can be a luxury, too.

Opportunity is a privilege. However, people have a hard time acknowledging that.

Liz Moor and Sam Friedman explain this internal conflict as trying to reconcile unearned gifts with a society that wants you to earn your upward mobility from hard work and merit. Moor and Friedman interviewed 27 new homeowners in London who purchased property with help from their family. Almost every respondent attempted to dilute the appearance of their privilege by "placing one's own background within the context of a much longer family history." The new homeowners told stories of their parents', grandparents', and even great-grandparents' humble beginnings, economic challenges, and journeys to wealth.[17] In other words, they tried to justify their privilege to fit within a socially acceptable narrative. For many, dealing with these conflicting feelings only adds to the pressure of out-earning, out-growing, and out-performing the long shadow of their wealthy families.

Learning savvy financial strategies is a privilege, too. Investing, taxes, compounding interest, and even how our time carries value that can be bought back by outsourcing tasks, are all dynamic concepts that were likely modeled at a younger age for people who grew up with means.

All these tangible and intangible privileges contribute to wealth pooling at the tops of societies.[18] So, you can imagine the

5. THE FAMILY

complexities when someone who may or may not realize they've been raised this way falls in love with someone who was not.

Crissy, Joshua's wife, was not. She was raised by a single mother whose mental health made it hard for them to maintain a safe place to live. Crissy graduated high school early so she could build herself a better life as soon as possible.

"A lot of my feelings with money have to do with independence, safety, and security... I wanted to be out of the care of other people so I could establish myself and feel like I could take care of myself." Crissy's always earned her own money. She feels like she has to.

At first, she had a hard time accepting gifts from Joshua's family—she worried about the strings attached. She insisted on putting her own money into their wedding, because it felt icky not to contribute. But as her life intertwined with Joshua's and her relationship with her in-laws and sister-in-law bloomed, she's softened towards receiving help.

I asked if she's ever breathed a sigh of relief over the comfort of finding this kind of security in her spouse's family. She said, "Intellectually, I think I could do that. But I don't feel safe in doing that, given who I am."

This feels like a good time to introduce you to the family. Not Joshua's family—they seem quite lovely—but The Family. The kind of family to watch out for.

The Family wants to control your relationship. There are couples who live under the thumb of The Family's generational wealth. The Family influences where you live, controls where they vacation, and even stipulates what they do for a living. Neither their adult children nor the "married ins" (i.e., their spouses) have little say. The Family's lifestyle has strings that are hard to untie.

This world is not foreign to me.

My dad's parents had wealth. Pop earned his money through construction and commercial real estate. They were not generous people—they were exacting with their wealth. They gave for the purpose of buying loyalty, and they dangled the carrot much more than they gave. I didn't understand it until I got older. Before then, I was a little girl who didn't know why her Gram told stories of the gifts she showered upon other children, or why she wore a necklace that had other children's names on it. I didn't know why I never received birthday cards but was supposed to say thank you for tax strategies I would someday benefit from. See, they created a trust for my college education, which everyone kind of acknowledged was to help my dad out more than me. All I heard was that if I was sweeter, if I was more affectionate, *if, if, if,* I would have received more.

So sure, I had privilege, but I also had baggage: their only grandchild was never enough for them. I was taught that giving money is how you love. Not giving money is how you withhold love.

The Family may also enable their adult children to have poor money habits, if they're perpetually bailing them out of bad situations. All this does is tighten the ties between them, strengthening the adult child's dependence on their resources.

"If a family is really enmeshed, meaning there's not healthy, clear boundaries on where one starts and the other ends, it can get really toxic," said Ashley Quamme, therapist and financial behavior specialist. "That can bleed over into the marital relationship and cause a whole lot of friction."

Allowing this level of influence over your life is a choice. One that, as Quamme said, carries a lot of emotional risk.

You and your partner need to know who you're receiving financial support from. Are you dealing with benevolent parents like Joshua's, who just want to help? Or are you dealing with The Family who will never let you forget it?

Chandler's grandfather, for example, sold his cardboard box factory for $100M. For the benefit of his ten grandchildren, he set up "the bank," a fund that carries certain stipulations to borrow or receive from. College and healthcare would be paid for, but

5. THE FAMILY

for the most part, Chandler and his wife Nicole live their lives without the bank. Meanwhile, some of his cousins don't even work. "We've always thought, we have to do this ourselves," he said. Not borrowing from his grandfather is a matter of pride for them. "I want my own legacy."

If there are stipulations attached to receiving money, you need to know them, understand them, and accept or reject them together. Expectations are everything with family wealth. You both need to agree, and the sooner, the better.

Speaking of agreements, I'm about to say something lawyer-ish. You've been warned.

Prenuptial agreements can be a useful tool for setting expectations when two people who come from disparate wealth backgrounds get married. A 2022 survey conducted by The Harris Poll found that 15% of Americans who have been married or are currently engaged signed a prenup, up from 3% in 2010. These numbers might feel low, but sentiment is shifting as more people understand all that prenups can accomplish.[19]

Back when divorce was taboo, the mere mention of a prenuptial agreement carried an assumption that you were planning for your marriage to fail. That's simply not the case anymore. Yes, they outline legal terms for what would happen if your marriage ends, but they can also outline the structure, frequency, and parameters around receiving financial support while you're married. They can even alleviate some of the adult child's insecurities around trusting their spouse. Of course, the "married-in" might feel weird having transactional discussions about their relationship, but having everyone's cards on the table up front is better than guessing what's on them later.

I considered placing a caveat here such as, "The agreement must be fair." There's a problem with that statement, though, because *fair* is relative, especially given the lopsided financial resources at each party's disposal.

What you need to seek is fairness in negotiations. If you're marrying into a family that insists upon a prenuptial agreement, *you need your own attorney*! (If I could print that on the book cover, I would.) Your attorney needs to be able to explain the financial terms on the table to you. And you need to be able to live with them. You need to believe they're worth it.

A fairytale arrangement becomes inherently unfair if you get lost in it. Allowing yourself to be subsumed by your partner's family puts you in a vulnerable financial and emotional position.

That's my primary concern: abandoning your career because you no longer "need" the money, then feeling purposeless years later. Or even worse, you divorce and are left with nothing.

"A lot of times, people stay married because they can't afford not to," said Jennifer Belmont Jennings, a trusts and estates attorney who also holds her CFP® certification. She believes in the power of building your personal wealth to offset the risk of that happening.

"If you have a marital plan in place where you are deliberate and intentional about accumulating wealth as a married couple *outside* of the family resources, that is going to help put you in a better position in the future should something happen."

You and your partner should have your own financial advisor separate and apart from who manages The Family's wealth. And as the partner marrying in, you absolutely need to be a part of those conversations—this professional is a resource to you, too. If you have opportunities to save cash gifts given to you, do that. And consider building your own investment portfolio. All these active efforts keep you dialed into your finances and can serve as a hedge should you ever need one.

Ashley Quamme takes a broader view of how to protect yourself: just keep getting better. There's immense value in developing skill sets and continuing to hone them over time. You don't need to be earning money from something right this second for it to

5. THE FAMILY

benefit you and your family. Your confidence and sense of purpose benefit you a lot.

The moral of this fairytale is that everyone should maintain a sense of self.

And they all lived happily ever after...

Sorry. We're not done.

Let's assume you've accepted your partner's family. They've accepted you. You know where the cards lie. You know who you are. That's all great, but as you'll read in the coming sections, you still have to navigate life as two people raised under very different conditions. How?

Identifying your common values will be your north star. Once you do, you'll be able to filter the finer details of your decisions through those values. Having an abundance of wealth won't replace them. In fact, you probably need your values even more when money isn't a factor.

I want you to think back to five minutes ago, when you were reading about the merit-loving, ladder-climbing narrative our society is obsessed with.

Across the socioeconomic spectrum, you will find so many couple's commonalities reduced to just that: *earning, stacking*, and *growing*. Now, imagine this doesn't need to be a priority in your life. What would it be then? Your children? Your faith? Social justice causes that matter to you?

My point is, people in this position have a huge opportunity to make it matter. That's a privilege you shouldn't waste.

I think about my legacy a lot. The money I received for college was held over my head for so long that I found it hard to locate my own gratitude for it. I couldn't stomach thanking Gram, and Pop was gone by then. I tell myself I honored his gift by working hard, having multiple jobs during school, doing my part. I'd like to think he'd be proud of me, his only granddaughter: the lawyer, the author, the damn good mother. But for too long, I was trying to out-earn the long shadow this cast over me.

I remember the last time we spoke.

He told me, the only thing that matters is my blood and my money. Nothing about love.

I wish he could read this book, so he could see how wrong that is.

6. WORDS WE CAN'T HEAR

Inheritances are more than dollars in an account. They look backward and forward at the same time.

Have you ever dreamed that you're speaking with someone, but then you wake up and can't remember the words?

The conversation seemed so real. You're grasping for what was said, but you can never quite figure it out.

Inheritances are like dreams we've woken up from. We look backward for their meaning and inward for their purpose, but we almost never hear the words we need.

Most inheritances aren't worth millions of dollars. They're five figures or less.*[20] And yet, money that won't alter the course of your life from a financial standpoint still wields so much power.

I asked Dr. Charles Eckhart why inheritances sometimes carry more emotional weight than other windfalls, such as bonuses we receive at work. He said, unlike sums we can attribute to our performance, we struggle with whether we're entitled to inheritances—whether we've *earned* them. Emotionally, that's a heavy load to bear.

"Inheritance is a numeric symbolic delivery of all you ever have left," he said. "Nobody gets everything they ever wanted of their loved ones. We all wish we had more time, we had more love, we had more understanding."

And that was when Dr. Eckhart made me cry. (I am only slightly embarrassed by this.)

It seems like almost all writing on inheritances and relationships is about insulating them from your spouse. Indeed, most legal scholarship focuses on how to protect your assets for an eventual divorce. I will tell you that inheritances are considered individual property in most states, so long as you keep them separately held,[21] but I'm just telling you to say I did. This all isn't the point.

People go on a journey when they inherit money. Some assign significant meaning to it. Others are afraid to touch it, as it's too infused with memories. Whether your departed loved ones set explicit expectations or not, inheritances force us to examine our past and our future at the same time. They cause us to ask questions we may never learn the answers to.

---

* A *Yahoo! Finance* article broke down the Federal Reserve's most recent Survey of Consumer Finances from 2016-2019, finding that data on American inheritances can be misleading. While the American household technically inherits $46,200 on average, that amount skews upward due to the top 10% of households, which are much more likely to receive six-figure inheritances. The next 40% of households receive an average inheritance of $45,900, while households below this income floor receive an average of four figures down to nothing at all.

6. WORDS WE CAN'T HEAR

No one should have to walk the journey of grief alone.

Yet, it's a delicate dance around the emotions attached to this money. Granting leeway to your grieving partner goes a long way but has its limits.

You are their partner, after all. Even if they're looking backwards, you are their present and their future.

Hallie's dad was a successful businessman in Beijing, frugal in lifestyle but meticulous with his finances. He made Hallie read *Rich Dad, Poor Dad* as a teen and play the CASHFLOW Board Game with her little brother. Neither struck a chord. Money was something she didn't take for granted but also knew would be there if she needed it.

She was more like her mom: a creative, a "do what you love, and the rest will come" type. But Hallie knew how to propose a plan, like the one asking her dad to pay for college and housing in New York City, where she'd eventually meet her now-wife, Jessica.

The oldest of five siblings, Jessica has always been a caretaker. She went to work at 13 to help her parents with the bills and hasn't stopped working since. She joined the Peace Corps and lived in Ethiopia. She gives and gives and gives.

She is meticulous with her finances. Hallie's father always liked her.

He fell ill before the pandemic and died in 2021. Before his health turned grave, he made sure Hallie met with his private advisor to go over his affairs. But living across the world posed its own set of challenges when Hallie realized she'd have to settle his estate in Taiwan.

The administrative burden of dying can weigh heavy on family members, even when there's a plan in place, said Jennifer Belmont Jennings, a trusts and estates attorney. "You have a family who's trying to grieve, and all they can think about is how to clean the mess."

Hallie flew to Taiwan to handstamp the paperwork, hold the

funeral, clean out his apartment, and decide what to do with his things. He left her investments and a property, which he covered the mortgage for. There were also some sandalwood trees in Asia and Malaysia, but no one can figure out what the deal is with those.

Looking back, she said, she had to block out the grief to get it all done. So, when she returned home, she didn't want to talk about it. She left her inheritance there, in Taiwan, managed by her dad's private advisor.

But Jessica felt something was off. The advisor was always moving money around, investing in things they didn't really agree with. Hallie didn't have good answers for why, and she shut down the conversation with Jessica.

"I didn't think about taking control of that, because I was like, well, this is the way he planned it. And I think this is how, you know, he would want me to deal with the money," she said.

She wasn't ready to ask those questions—the ones without answers.

"One has to mourn what was lost to be able to access the money and see it as capital rather than a symbolic representation of the wish to heal up all the pain," said Dr. Charles Eckhart.

Grief finds you in the quiet moments. Sitting in the car, trying on clothes, staring at numbers in a bank account.

You can't decide when grief begins or ends. Grief finds you.

Be gentle with your partner's grief, but recognize there might be a time to step in.

Around tax time the following year, Jessica was no longer comfortable with how much she didn't know.

"What I said to Hallie was, this is the money your dad gave you. And it's yours. If you want to keep it for yourself, I'm not going to be angry." But she didn't even know how much was there—the investments weren't in U.S. dollars and the statements weren't in English. She also didn't know whether Hallie had to pay taxes for

6. WORDS WE CAN'T HEAR

assets overseas, which Jessica typically handled for the household. Would this money change their lives just a little, or forever?

Jessica was right. You should never assume that money your partner inherits belongs to you, too. If she's still wading through grief, that presumption alone could hurt her.

But it's not unreasonable to want to know what's there. Set expectations early on if you anticipate a meaningful inheritance coming your way, because your emotions may cloud your judgment when the time comes. In the event you are financially struggling as a household, it's not unreasonable to use it.

As with faith, grief carries otherworldly reflection. But you still have to swim.

Hallie filled Jessica in. They moved the money to the United States and hired a new financial advisor. In time, Hallie realized her father would want them to use the inheritance together.

Jessica is a caretaker. This is Hallie's way to care for her, too.

7. THE HARDEST WORK

Childhood trauma can impact so much, but how you cope is not who you are.

The whole point of starting here, with the people and places and events that shaped you, is for you to honor and understand where you have been. Then, you can honor and understand where your partner has been.

In relationships, self-awareness is a threshold burden put on us all—not an enigma for your loved ones to sort out. We all have our own work to do, though it's true, some of us have more work than others.

What does it mean to *honor* your past? The past chapters showed you some ways but not all of them. There are times from your past you do not wish to honor; not in the traditional sense of being "humbled and honored," a cliché glaze over what you lived

7. THE HARDEST WORK

through to get here. Some stories we wish weren't ours. Some pain is not all for the best.

I think that to *honor* our past is also to accept the bad things we can't change; acknowledge how they've manifested in our adult lives; and find the fortitude to heal from them. There is more honor in this work than our "humbled and honored" work.

Trauma, as a concept, wears many hats. Instances of adult financial trauma—declaring bankruptcy, losing your job, weathering a recession, incurring debt, and more—appear throughout this book, and we'll examine how couples' abilities to process the emotional distress from these major events impacts the dynamics of their relationships.

But for now, let's look back to when we were young.

Some of us experienced things we couldn't fully understand while they were happening. As kids, that's fair. We could barely color inside the lines—how could we possibly connect the dots?

According to the Center for Disease Control, about 64% of adults in the United States report they've experienced an adverse childhood experience (ACE), which could be any of a whole host of traumatic events that occur before the age of 18.[22] Examples include but aren't limited to abuse, violence at home or in your community, the death (or near death) of a parent, homelessness, food insecurity, or domestic instability due to your parents getting divorced, separated, or incarcerated. We need not leap to see the tie between these events and your mental health. But in fact, people who had ACEs are likely to experience financial stress as adults, too.[23]

The more stories that people shared with us, the more I grew to hate labels like "Big T" and "Little t" trauma. From a clinician's standpoint, I can see how the distinction might matter, but through a lay person's eyes, pain is pain. Your story is your story. Childhood trauma impacts your feelings and behaviors around money in adulthood regardless of income levels. I make this point not to diminish those who have lived through the worst, but to normalize the impact on others who have buried it, hidden from it, or told themselves, "You're successful, though, so it all worked out."

Aja Evans, who you met earlier, is an expert on how trauma impacts your finances. She told me that after you experience trauma, you're always looking out for it again. That's why you form defense mechanisms and coping skills to make you feel safe.

Children who went without food, for example, might never throw out their leftovers. Children exposed to death or violence might not save for retirement, because they can't imagine a world they get to grow old in.

We saw versions of this in our interviews. Amy watched her parents fight incessantly over money as a child and refuses to share credit cards with her husband. Walter, now in his fifties, *still* works to unpack the financial trust issues he inherited from his parents' bitter, protracted divorce. But no one's childhood story struck me quite like David's.

Let me tell you about David. He became a Division I athlete, United States Naval Academy graduate, mathematician, cryptologist, and robotics surgeon. At 35, he'd achieved more accolades than many will ever. But these wins only tell the story of now.

David remembers when his dad left. He told him, you're the man of the house—take care of your family. With his mother in and out of the hospital for her mental health, David and his brother faced homelessness, couch surfing on good nights and sleeping in a car on others. Eating Pizza Hut on good nights and feeling hungry on others. Getting beaten. Walking in the rain. As David came up in life, he wore that pressure on his shoulders: *take care of them*, and he did.

"There was a time, because of the way my life went, where I wasn't afraid to die, because I wasn't really living," he told us. "Then, it became, I can't fail, because I don't have anything else to go back to."

7. THE HARDEST WORK

Trying to emotionally process having money and relative stability for the first time is not the easiest road to walk. David told us three things he needed to feel safe back then: a car, a roof over his head, and a refrigerator full of food. But as early earners, he and his brother both overspent on groceries. He owned 30 pairs of jeans. He needed to have a certain amount in his checking account to feel safe, but at one point, opened 17 credit cards to maintain that. These decisions were David's armor—his ways to cope.

I spoke with Ed Coambs, CFP® and couples therapist, about how money can become a substitute for our unmet needs from childhood. As a result of early trauma, people might have a hard time making financial decisions, feeling confident in their achievements, assessing risks, and even collaborating with their partner.

Money was tight during David's residency, and he had his wife, Kim, and their children to think about, too. He started learning about personal finance and became much more of an intentional spender and investor. But at the same time, he just kept working, reaching higher and higher. Kim, a nurse practitioner, didn't come from much but had something David didn't: a two-parent household, a solid family, unrestricted love. She knows the value of his time. His health. His presence for their kids.

He told her, "I need you to protect me from me, because if not, I'll just continue. I'm just going to think we don't have enough."

Maybe David wasn't climbing—he was running.

David didn't really understand what it meant to celebrate or even allow someone else to take care of him. No one had ever taken care of him, let alone given him permission to take proper care of himself. But he told us, "I love her, and I had to learn to see what she saw."

Now, they go on family vacations. They unplug. They invest in themselves (and the markets!) without the fear of it all going away. They can do that for their family, because David is no longer making financial decisions for the person he no longer is.

Maybe we can't stop running until we feel safe where we are.

I couldn't connect the dots in my own life—not until now.

As a kid, each day felt like a moment before a moment. Anxiety ran deep in me, not rooted in one thing but everything that could go wrong. My little life was filled with "what if's" that sucked joy from simple pleasures, like playing in the deep corners of a field or riding my bike beyond the bend. Watching planes fly overhead, I'd worry they'd drop right down on my head. When my parents went out for the night, I'd worry they'd never come home.

I always had this thing about my parents dying. Maybe it's a common fear in only children; that or I just watched the movie *Annie* too many times. But I look back now and wonder where anxiety ends and fortuity begins. There's a whole lot of questions you ask yourself about the event that changed the course of your life.

There was a double-line road five minutes from my house. My dad was there, and we had to get there. Maybe my shoes were still in my sleepover duffel, or a closet—there wasn't time to find the right shoes. My mom looked as if there wasn't time.

We pulled up to the flares blocking the road, and she ran. I shivered in my nightgown, not knowing where to be.

I assessed the scene. A Mercedes Benz unscathed on the wrong side of the road. White shrapnel, the remains of our Ford Explorer, clung to a tree.

My dad did not die, but he came close enough. After a long time in the hospital, they brought a double-wide medical bed into our den where the couch usually was. We spent time together in that bed, operating it up and down. He liked the cartoons I'd draw on his leg casts, hours-long projects I took great care with. I'd like to think

7. THE HARDEST WORK

that while he healed, we spent more time together than before the accident, but that could just be me overdramatizing things.

Maybe I just paid closer attention to him, not as a mainstay figure in my life but as a person. Someone who could go somewhere and never come back, by his own volition or by God's. I watched him grapple with this heavy truth before any 11-year-old girl could know what it means.

He wouldn't talk much about the details, like the height of the driver's seat saving his life, causing the truck to collapse around his legs instead of his vital organs. Or the unlikelihood that my mom would have survived, had she been in the passenger's seat. Had she not had an inkling I'd want to come home early from my sleepover. Had she driven the truck and left him with the sedan. So many variables. He didn't have to talk about them, because the moments before that moment lived on his face for a long time.

Our den closed in, its dense brown walls hovering over him. Everything would change. The life we had together was alright but not *enough*.

We almost lost him. Then we helped him get better, and we lost him all the same.

My parents separated less than two years after the accident. There's no use in assigning empty adjectives to how we felt—there's not enough space for that here.

What I took from it was a toxic belief that your life's biggest challenge will arise, and you will need to overcome it alone. No one else can help you. In fact, everyone who loves you will need to grip onto whatever's left of you, and it will tear them apart.

I didn't realize this was part of my money story. Their divorce, sure, but not this. I told myself I was happy for him to go live out his enough. Now, I know that was just my first attempt to cope.

As I watched him sort out his life from the sidelines, money was our only bond together. The only way I could say I needed him and the only way he was available to answer. It was all he could give. It was all I could receive.

Bringing a partner into the darker moments of your past can feel impossible. Not because you want to hide, *per se*, but because it takes a certain softness to accept the role that childhood trauma plays in your adult life. It's easier to bury it. It's easier to talk about expensive dinners and credit cards and harder to talk about fathers.

"It's so difficult for two people to talk about money," Aja Evans told me, "Because what they're saying is, I'm going to put myself in a position of vulnerability to tell you this information, and I need to trust that you can hold it and not judge me at the same time."

How we cope is not who we are.

A partner coping with past trauma has to ask themselves, are the circumstances I've faced still present in my life? Are they still true today? Many of us get trapped in stories we can't see the end of, because we need help writing the ending.

Given the prevalence, Ed Coambs explained that he looks for childhood trauma in all the couples he works with as a financial therapist. "If I don't ask about it, it's not going to be revealed," he said. People need to break their own misconceptions that they don't have trauma in their lives, especially if they're in a serious relationship with someone who does. There might be more to explore about the emotional patterns tying them together.

I asked him whether all financial therapy should be couples therapy.

If you're married, his answer is yes.

"You're both equally responsible for the dynamic that's being created," Coambs said. "If one partner starts getting healthier and healthier in their relationship with money, it's going to upset the balance in the relationship."

7. THE HARDEST WORK

But, like everything else you've read in *Beginnings* about discovering and acknowledging your partner's full background, you've got to show up in a constructive way. Doubling down on their parents or any other culprits of their pain might feel good in the short term, but it's hardly helpful for their healing process. People have mixed emotions about their families. Inserting yourself into that murkiness risks making it worse.

"You as a partner might need to release your partner's parents for the pain and consequences *you're* now experiencing in your relationship," he said.

None of this is easy.

Even if opening these doors takes more time than anything you've ever done together, be patient. You may need time and trust and the help of third-party resources like therapists to unlock them. That's to be expected, because in separating your or your partner's behaviors from what's in your hearts, you're doing the hardest work. Honorable work.

"What I'm always trying to convey is that there are no good guys or bad guys," Coambs said. "There are no devils or angels. There are just humans."

Some of the stories you will read in the coming sections might make you question that statement. But just remember, we all started the same: our feet, our hands, our parents' faces.

It's the world that finds us all.

YOUR QUESTIONS ON BEGINNINGS

1. When did you first become aware of money?
2. How did it make you feel?
3. Who handled the finances in your family growing up?
4. Were your parents good with money?
5. Has anything from your past shaped the way you approach money?
6. What values do you hold close to your heart, and where do they come from?
7. Does anyone else's money influence your life?
8. How do you feel about receiving financial gifts?

PART II.
MISTAKES

What a negative word. A heavy one that carries feelings on its back. *Mistakes*. I know what you're thinking, but I promise, we're not about to tell you that everything you do is wrong.

Quite the contrary. We're less interested in the financial decisions you make than how you make them—and when they're wrong, how you move through them. Mistakes can present opportunities to learn more about each other, deepen trust, become nimble, and gain better perspective on your lives. That, or they can totally screw things up. No big deal!

We are going to look at every angle of mistakes. First, how they happen. Mistakes can be quick or a slow trickle over time. You may not know how to right the ship, because once upon a time you both agreed to something, or you've been doing it so long you don't know any other way.

Besides, what even is a mistake?

You already know from Part One that the stories we tell ourselves about money matter. Not all those stories live in the past—we write new ones every day. One person's biggest mistake could be a blip to someone else. Knowing how bad your partner feels about a decision they've made gives you the best insight into supporting them.

We will separate mistakes from stuff that just isn't that deep. Like the photos in your first Facebook album, you should be allowed to get it wrong without paying for it forever. (Does this age me? So be it.) How you talk about minor transgressions, like a small credit card balance, has a great impact on the confidence you'll need to have a voice in your joint finances.

Confidence matters, but at the same time, the way you think can lead to mistakes, too. Never being satisfied is a chronic ailment, which will always find its way into your relationship. So is wishing for something so badly, you let magic consume the truth.

Lastly, on truth. Some people don't tell the truth, and those mistakes are harder to forgive. You will read about walking away. You will read about staying, too.

8.
THE CROISSANT

*Some mistakes don't
happen in an instant.
They compound over time.*

The easiest time to judge a quarterback is on Monday morning, when you're analyzing what went right or wrong the day before. It's easy to point out what you or anyone should have done when you're playing the tape back.

But most decisions don't come with a rewind button.

At the time, you have to make a choice based on what you see. There are lots of moving parts. You trust your gut; maybe, you go with your heart. Whether you are right or wrong, you can't go backwards. There's no do-overs when the game's already over. All you can do is try again.

Mistakes don't only happen in a snap—they can materialize over time. This rings true for the financial choices you make in your relationship: you could have plotted the whole thing out. You could have had the best of intentions and agreed wholeheartedly.

Still, years later, you might find yourselves looking back and asking, what the hell were we thinking?

If you're wondering what the catalyst for such a sudden change of heart could be, I will tell you: anything. Anything can be the last straw, and it's probably not as sudden as you think. Years of little choices build a tall, shaky tower that can topple over and become a huge deal. All it takes is one measly croissant from 7-Eleven.

Yes, you read that right. Let me introduce you to Henry and Chloe.

When we first spoke with them, they were in Bangkok. Next, they were in Denmark. Henry and Chloe travel the world, two creatives who value pursuing life outside the limits of regular office hours. They found each other in art school, but like the couples you met in *Beginnings*, come from very different places. Henry hailed from a working-class family in Northern England that never spoke about money, leaving him to sort it out on his own. Chloe grew up an ex-pat in Singapore, where her father did well in the shipping industry, but she had a hard time finding work as a teen due to student visa restrictions. Chloe hated not having the freedom to earn her own money. Her mother relied on her father's income, and she really didn't want that for herself.

Just three months into dating, Chloe's family offered Henry a place to stay in their family home in London. Chloe's father was moving out (as in, divorce) and they felt better having a man in the house. Henry needed the help but was adamant in showing Chloe and her family that he wasn't using her for her money.

So, he proposed they split everything.

I mean, *everything*.

Each week or so, the couple reconciled their joint purchases—from groceries all the way down to cups of coffee—on a spreadsheet Henry created and then split them 50/50 with money from their separate bank accounts.

"Money's easy. It's numerical. It's divisible. It goes on a spreadsheet," he thought. "I believed it was coming from a good place and would lead to a good place," he said.

So much comes from a good place.

8. THE CROISSANT

Jenny Olson researches consumer financial decision-making as an assistant professor with Indiana University's Kelley School of Business. She and her partnering scholars randomly assigned joint, separate, or "do as you wish" accounts to engaged and newlywed couples to study the impact that account structures have on the health of a relationship in its most impressionable time. They found that couples who merged money in a joint account sustained a stronger relationship, whereas the others faced a steady, standardized decline over a two-year period.[24]

Better accountability and communication are two ways that joint accounts benefit a relationship. But in the context of Henry and Chloe's setup, a third reason interested me more.

Relationships should be communal. "Partners can respond to each other's needs," Olson told me. "There is no expectation of repaying with future favors."

Olson likened it to other kinds of responsibilities: no one wants a romantic partner who keeps score of who took out the trash or who did the kids' bath time how many nights in a row. That's not how you take care of another person. What Henry and Chloe were doing was less communal and more of an exchange, like a business relationship.

"It's very tit for tat," Olson said. "You pat my back, and I'll pat yours."

Which is not to say there aren't valid reasons for keeping separate accounts, or splitting expenses a certain way, or coming up with any arrangement you both think is fair. In practice, Douglas tells his clients to do what works for them, but to be hyper-aware of how easily feelings can change.

In Henry and Chloe's case, they were not yet married. They were living in her family's home. They both had their reasons for agreeing to the plan. After five years, they even opened a joint account to make reconciling their expenses easier than using the spreadsheet. But they were still splitting hairs. And after eight years, the deal had run its course.

One late night in Japan, after many drinks, they wandered into a 7-Eleven. Henry picked up an extra croissant, and Chloe absolutely lost it. (I was told, he always eats more.)

She screamed that he was the one benefitting the most from their so-called 50/50 split. "It's not fair, you know?" she told him. "You're not walking the walk."

In the sober light of day, she felt bad for exploding, but not about what she said. She didn't want to "fix" the 50/50 split by telling Henry to just eat less or start itemizing even more. The whole system was broken.

"Where does it end?" she said. "If I have a sip of your drink, does that mean that I owe you, like, two pennies or whatever?"

"She was absolutely right," Henry realized. "There was something fundamentally wrong."

I still wondered, why the croissant? Why was *that moment*, after eight years, the moment when Chloe could no longer hold back her resentment?

That's when I found out, Chloe's job was in jeopardy. Until then, they had pretty much earned the same amount of money, but faced with the threat of that changing, her slight grievances over appetizers and drinks and convenience store baked goods didn't seem so trivial anymore.

The thing that altered how she felt about their plan was life. Life happened.

Two people might not realize they need to make changes at the same time. You might be the first to realize that the way you share expenses, invest, or save, is the wrong way. That *wrong* way might have once been the *right* way, but now, it's not. Bringing this up to your partner is harder than it seems, even for spouses who communicate well.

"I think it takes a ton of courage to sit down with the person that

8. THE CROISSANT

you're trying to build a life with and bring up what you might be messing up," said Dr. Victoria Elf Raymond, a licensed marriage and family therapist and clinical sexologist. There's usually a reason you're uncomfortable initiating that conversation.

Talking about money is inherently vulnerable, but trying to fix how you approach money is like stripping down naked and getting dressed all over again. Dr. Raymond says that some people find it harder to talk about than sex.

"So much depends on how much judgment you think your partner will place upon you, whether we're talking about your money beliefs or your sexual preferences," she said. "The difficulty comes from the story you tell yourself about how your partner will perceive you."

Imagine approaching your partner with: *I don't like the way we've been having sex for the past eight years.* Awkward. I know.

Yet, I can feel how close this admission is to: *I don't like the way we've been splitting our expenses for the past eight years.* They both challenge something private and personal you do together.

You got here slowly. You can correct course slowly, too. Dr. Raymond suggests you try something new before dismantling your whole operation. For example, if you're worried about commingling your funds, try saving for a new goal together first. When you combine to create abundance, you can see how working together helps you accomplish something you both want.

Henry and Chloe project abundance—not in material things but in their perspectives about work, life, travel, what they deem important. From where we sat across the Zoom screen, their approach to money didn't align with who they are or who they wish to be. Henry agreed.

"With our money, we were doing things that we thought were under the right framework, but we realized not just that you don't have to follow the framework, but the framework is all in your head," he said. "You can literally conceive something completely different that actually works for you rather than what you *think* should work for you."

After the blowup, they began working through it, and they still are. Finding a way forward is almost never a one-time change and all of a sudden, everything's gravy. Change takes time. Trial and error. Collaboration.

For starters, they're buying each other things without the expectation of being paid back. "When we cover certain things now, it comes from a place of giving and generosity," Chloe said.

I love that their new mindset transcends finance and impacts how they approach chores and responsibilities around the house, too. More on that later.

"It's a complete paradox that aiming for fairness led us to feeling like things were unfair," said Henry. "Stop trying to be so fair and just buy someone a coffee."

Or, you know, a croissant.

9.
DIABLO

*Mistakes live in the stories
we tell ourselves.*

I've been writing about overcoming student loan debt since my late twenties. Over time, the story's changed. What does it mean to *overcome* something, anyway? Do you gain control over it? Rid yourself of it? Forgive yourself for it?

What you tell yourself about a certain set of facts might be completely different than what someone else would.

Mistakes can be subjective. You embody them each your own.

In the United States, 42.7 million borrowers harbor a $1.7 trillion federal student loan debt balance.[25] Many students had no choice but to borrow money for higher education, but whether they'll say it was worth it depends on who you ask. According to a 2023 *Bankrate* survey, nearly a quarter of people regret taking on too much student loan debt. More than two-thirds of survey participants would've changed *something*: they would've sought out more scholarships; worked more during school; attended somewhere more affordable; or gone to community college.[26] I raise this point just to highlight how we all walk away with our own takes on this decision.

Let me show you how different two people's feelings about the same decision can be.

When we first met Adam and his wife, Diane, I quickly realized our paths were similar. We both earned our undergrad degrees from state universities. We both wanted high-income careers. We both believed the pamphlets and statistics telling us that law school would get us there. We both graduated as the global economy collapsed.

We both borrowed more than $200,000. And that's where our similarities end.

Adam realized on the first day of law school he didn't want to be a lawyer. He just wanted the skill set and would use his law degree as an investment to gain admission to his dream MBA program at Notre Dame. Him and Diane were just married and living long distance, a less-than-ideal setup they'd have to extend to make it happen.

"It was obviously a big conversation as we went into marriage," Diane said about her sacrifices for Adam's two graduate degrees. "But Adam's an adult in the room. He has a very good head on his shoulders. And I 100% trusted that if he thought this was a worthy investment, then great. I'm along for the ride."

In my case, the money I borrowed for law school wasn't just a decision. It was The Decision: the riskiest bet I'd ever made; a next step for a millennial who ran out of steps; a projection of my fantasy to outearn my late grandfather; a path to rely on my divorced parents less; a conflicting cry for my dad's attention. These are the hidden stakes of a decision—the ones you don't mention. You'd probably never have to unless something went wrong.

Law school was a gauntlet even before the wheels came off the financial system. When they did, our high-paying job prospects vanished faster than a credit default swap, those employment stats

9. DIABLO

a piece of history frozen in time. Like Adam, I had my doubts about lawyering; but unlike Adam, I'd never admitted them. *This is the bed you made*, I thought. *Time to lie down.*

I asked Adam if he had regrets. He also entered the workforce on the heels of the Great Recession, facing job insecurity and a daunting student loan repayment schedule. Life came at us quick.

"To be honest with you, I had a fair amount of guilt around it," he said. "I saw those payments, and I saw how hard we were working professionally, and I saw how much was going towards debts I had taken on. Diane never made me feel like, *you did this*, or *boy would our lives be easier without it*. But I internalized that and felt it."

Adam and Diane used their discomfort to form an aggressive plan to pay it back. They tightened their lifestyle and downsized their apartment. They lived on one salary and used the other just for loans. By 2016, they paid them back. And no, they don't regret it.

"We took a non-math approach," he joked.

"Totally non-math," she agreed. "It was all heartfelt feelings behind it."

After our conversations, I thought about them a lot. How could they position Adam's student loans as a challenge to conquer, while I thought of mine as the biggest money regret of my life?

"Mistakes are based on the stories we tell ourselves," said Dr. Megan McCoy, an associate professor at Kansas State University's Department of Financial Planning. Regrets can just be hurdles "if you use them as part of a story of peace and well-being around your finances."

Through that lens, Adam and Diane could have had any amount of student loan debt and still framed their mission around sacrifice, teamwork, and purpose. In their story, Adam's student loan debt was "pure evil," a sadistic villain they'd annihilate together. They nicknamed their account with the earmarked funds... Diablo. I'm serious.

My debt wasn't a villain. It wasn't some monster like Godzilla that I could plan for and attack. My debt was me. It was everything I wasn't: the jobs I couldn't get. The approval I desired. The love that felt an arm's length away.

Brené Brown writes and presents extensively on the difference between guilt and shame.[27] Guilt, like what Adam described above, is constructive. Using guilt to hold yourself accountable, you can remedy or improve upon the decisions you make. Brown says, guilt means "I made a mistake." Shame is "I am a mistake."

The first expert I interviewed for this book who used the word "shame" sent a shiver through my body. The word washed over me. I could feel it everywhere.

I was deep in shame at my second job at an international law firm, where I worked on insurance coverage lawsuits stemming from catastrophic events like oil spills and crane collapses. It felt like they owned me. I'd never felt so small.

I walked home through the streets of Midtown Manhattan at all hours of the night, music pumping through my corded headphones with another soundtrack on top: my words, to myself. *You are worthless. You deserve this.* I began idealizing dark things. Not death, but pain. I wondered if I could just get a little hurt... anything for a way out.

You'd be shocked how many people reach this point. Way more than will admit it.

Shame is more than a funk. Shame is a fog.

Lazetta Braxton, CFP®, explained to me how shame can place you in a money "FOG," where you can't see clearly beyond the Fear, Obligation, and Guilt inside. You can become angry at the wrong things, like my debt, or even money in general. But it's a deflection from what you're really feeling. The issues we face aren't the money's fault.

"Money is neutral," she said. "It's the energy you give it that makes it come to life."

It took Douglas a while to realize how deep my shame cut, but

9. DIABLO

he can't be blamed for that. I spent the entirety of law school pushing him away. By the time I hit rock bottom, we were young adults living together. It was like getting to know each other all over again.

He waited to propose until I found a new job. He said he wanted me to rediscover the hope I could become the person I wanted to be. We agreed I should take a lower-paying corporate job that was simpler and more sustainable—higher loan payments could wait. I got promoted and started to rebuild my confidence, brick by brick.

The first time I overcame debt was when I learned I was in control. Douglas taught me that.

Four years later, we received an unexpected opportunity. A regional bank started a program to privately refinance graduate student loan debt from high-potential borrowers at a fraction of the interest rate. Only certain degrees qualified, like Douglas's MBA from New York University.

After refinancing his debt with the bank, we asked them to consider mine. They agreed, but only if he would co-sign the loan. (There's probably more to say about that, but I digress.) Douglas didn't even hesitate.

In hindsight, this meant more to our relationship than the ring he knelt down with on the steps of Lincoln Center. His actions said, *I am here. Your burdens are my burdens. You don't need to walk this life alone. And also, I believe in you.*

Douglas's decision managed to change every bit of how I thought about my student loans. I no longer romanticized this idea that the day they'd disappear would be the day my life began. Our interest payments shrunk so sizably, I started to see how other relationships with debt could exist.

The second time I overcame debt was when I wasn't afraid of it anymore. In a very tangible way, Douglas gave me that.

But mistakes are still subjective. Healing from them is, too.

What one person needs to hear, needs to see, needs to do, might be completely different than the next. If you love someone who is trying to figure this out, you should want to help them do it.

Maybe your partner just needs someone to slay the dragon with, like Adam and Diane. Or maybe, the feelings run much deeper. As a partner, you can't wipe their shame away, but you can create space for vulnerable conversations that open the door to understanding what they need to make it hurt less. Once you know what those conditions are, you can tailor your support—financial and otherwise—to help them heal.

The third and final time I overcame debt was forgiving myself. Douglas didn't do that, but he made it possible.

10. MISTAKES VERSUS MISSTEPS

Letting go of the little things is critical to your confidence.

Heroes aren't who they used to be. As early as the first recorded mythological texts, humans told the stories of superhuman characters of the utmost strength, morality, and courage. Medieval times brought about the chivalrous hero, a gendered ideal driven by a duty to protect and perhaps tussle in a sword fight or two—maybe with horses. Wartime heroes earned their stature on the battlefield, revered for their sacrifice and valor in their commitment to country. Pop culture heroes like Superman taught us to believe in magic and ourselves. In recent years, the pandemic made unexpected heroes out of ordinary people who bravely showed up.

I don't have a problem with calling any of these real or fictitious people heroes. My issue's with everyone else. The media creates these narrative arcs that glorify good and bad actors alike for attention. We worship the wrong people because they're entertaining, even if their hijinks carry a dangerous message. Then, we've got social media overdramatizing the everyday nothings of life—anyone can start to believe they're a hero when enough people call them one. *Hero Packs Lunch for his Children. Hero Brings Hungover Friend Iced Coffee.* I've seen the label used in dumber contexts than these.

A hero needs someone to protect, teach, or inspire. Through the wide and contextual lens of time, that has mostly been the case, and a noble one at that. But these days, I'm not so sure. I think it's too easy to call yourself a hero. I worry, too many self-appointed heroes are convinced their partners need saving.

This is a chapter about mistakes that aren't ones. Some of these not-so-great decisions are *something*, but they are not a big enough deal to hold over your partner's head.

Of all the regrettable choices couples mentioned to us in their interviews, credit card debt was the most common. A *U.S. News & World Report* survey showed that almost 45% of respondents had existing credit card debt before they attempted to pay for a wedding.[28] That's nearly one in two. One partner brings credit card debt into a relationship almost as often as they don't.

There's a certain stigma around credit card debt. Talking heads in financial media regularly associate consumer debt with a spending problem, but that's such a cliché. Not all people who end up in credit card debt get there due to a lack of responsibility or control. They may not have even been spending on themselves, as women in particular bear the brunt of supporting their household's perpetual inventory lists. You'll read more about *that* invisible load later. But for now, let's accept as true that not everyone with debt has a spending problem.

Some people just learn an important lesson one time. Maybe they didn't understand what interest was, or they were young and stupid and breaking shit because that's what people do. My friends and I talk a lot about the reckless things we did in our twenties:

10. MISTAKES VERSUS MISSTEPS

all the cars we shouldn't have gotten into; all the trivial fights that jeopardized great friendships. We all wanted a piece of the drama, and that meant getting in too deep with all sorts of things, including money.

Mark, now a financial advisor in his thirties, admitted he was "kind of an idiot with money" when he lived in Los Angeles in his twenties: "I said yes to everything. I was a yes man. I loved to have fun and whatever the cost, I'd just float it." Bachelor parties, weddings, dating, the costs added up. Allie, one half of another couple we interviewed, was an *American Idol* fangirl who spent a whole lot of her twenties following season seven winner David Cook on tour around the country! She racked up $12,000 in credit card debt but doesn't regret it, *per se*. Now with a mortgage, husband, and two kids, she said, "I'm never going to be able to be that irresponsible again."

We can all shake our heads at our younger selves. Were your YOLO moments so bad if you came out unscathed with a life lesson under your belt?

When I asked Lazetta Braxton, CFP®, to speak with me about mistakes, she was wary. She doesn't like "mistakes." The word feels too final. It carries too much weight.

But when you "misstep," you're still moving.

"Maybe you've gone in the wrong direction or made a decision that didn't move you forward, but a misstep allows you to pivot," she explained.

Not all missteps are mistakes. You are allowed to just keep going.

Let's move past the bad decisions people make when living out their teenage dreams and get serious. Many people are out of options when they turn to a credit card. People lose jobs without emergency funds. They have children too young or need to escape tough living conditions. Unexpected medical debt can be devastating. I can describe tons of difficult financial circumstances that are just that: circumstantial. The only way through might be credit, and that's not your mistake—it's just a step in the wrong direction.

Shannah Game, CFP® and author of *Unraveling Your Relationship with Money*, believes that when we strive for perfection with our money, we set benchmarks we'll inevitably fall short of. Some of Shannah's coaching clients come to her looking for a playbook. "I want to explain there isn't one," she said. We all learn as we go. Some of us are more fortunate to learn those lessons with less financial blowback than others, but did a credit card help you put food on the table for your kids? Did it help you pay the rent when you lost work? Did it get you to the next place you needed to be?

If you answer, *yes*, then it wasn't a mistake.

Now tell me how your partner talks about your missteps. Are they letting you move on?

In some instances, the people we spoke with didn't seem like they were. One spouse—often a woman—would speak of her financial past, and she'd talk about her husband bailing her out: paying off the credit card debt; covering her rent; putting her on a budget. He would nod along with an air of *yup, I did that.*

I get it, though. No one wants someone they love to fall onto physical, emotional, or financial hard times. They'd want to fix whatever they can.

When I was under the darkest clouds of my student loan debt, Douglas was my knight who swooped in on his horse, i.e., the New York City subway system, and peeled me off the ground. He is a natural fixer, as many partners are. I used to say that he saved me—my words, not his. But almost 15 years later, I look back aghast at the shell of a person I was. I am thankful he's not a man who would capitalize on my most vulnerable moment and give it a continuing presence in our relationship to maintain an upper hand over me.

This is why the distinction between a mistake and a misstep is so

10. MISTAKES VERSUS MISSTEPS

important: not only because of the way you speak to yourself, but the way your partner speaks to you, too.

Falling on tough times doesn't make you bad with money. Being young and foolish doesn't mean you'll stay that way forever. Don't let anyone, especially your spouse, aggrandize what occurred.

The bedrock of an equitable relationship isn't built with knights and damsels, saviors and victims. You are both allowed to need. You are both allowed to help. And after you've survived, you both need to let it go.

For her clients, Game suggests this financial forgiveness exercise to help them do just that. Take 15 minutes to write out the money missteps you think you've made. Start with yours, because what you're projecting comes from your own internal thoughts and patterns. But you should do your partner's, too. Then, destroy them. Shred, cut, burn—bring that drama. The physical act of removing these micro-transgressions from your purview might remove them from your lives.

You don't need a partner to save you from your money. You need confidence.

When it comes to a gender gap in financial literacy, it's well-documented that women perceive they know less than men. In the 2021 Federal Reserve Board's Survey of Household Economics and Decisionmaking (SHED), respondents were asked three standard financial literacy questions. Half of the respondents were provided with the option of "don't know" as an answer.

When given the chance, women were much more likely to select "don't know." In fact, when asked a question about diversification, 20% more women selected "don't know" than men. But without the "don't know" option available to them, women and men scored *almost the same* on that question.[29] The only difference between the two: an option to tap out. Confidence.

When we spoke with men who purported to "rescue" their female spouses, they were quite often less involved in their finances than she should be, even years later. Matt and Mackenzie, for example, acknowledged how similar their dynamic was to his parents'. His father gave his mother and his two older half-sisters a better life. When Matt helped Mackenzie in their mid-twenties with her credit card debt, he said he felt compelled to do it, similar to the duty his father took on: "It's not like I was trying to be her sugar daddy right off the top, but I said, let me help you out. I'll take care of it. So, I definitely think there was a parallel there." Matt's mother stayed home to care for him and his siblings, but she handled the monthly finances. He wants that for Mackenzie, but she didn't seem so sure.

"I've seen the spreadsheet many times, and so I definitely know what it looks like and what the ranges are for things, but I am just not a numbers person at all," she said. "So, I stay far away from it." Mackenzie doesn't think she could handle their finances if something happened to Matt. That's not an intelligence problem—it's a confidence problem.

Which is why when your partner mischaracterizes your misstep as a bigger deal, it can become a bigger deal. Their message may signal to you that you were not savvy enough, strong enough, smart enough, to have handled it on your own. That you are not capable of handling money now.

The consequence of that message is you believing it.

Most people don't need a hero to save them. They just need to believe they can save themselves.

11.
THE THIRSTIEST

When nothing you have is ever enough, the people you love start to feel like moving targets.

Some people, they say, see a glass as half full. Others see a glass as half empty. My husband is a glass-half-full guy. Admittedly, I can be a bit of a downer, even with perspective on how blessed we are. But I don't believe people's outlooks are limited to *half full* and *half empty*. Some people don't even notice when their glass fills up, because they're too busy looking for a bigger one.

Thinking like this can consume your relationship with work, money, purpose, and the people you love.

Financial well-being expert Manisha Thakor wrote her book *Money Zen: The Secret to Finding Your "Enough"* to help people overcome the narrative that they always need more. Thakor herself was an admitted workaholic. For years, to the point of falling ill, she prioritized her career ambitions and net worth over everything. She tethered how she felt about herself to "flawed self-worth anchors," like her prized closet of designer handbags, one of many armors she hid behind.

"Whether it's the car you drive or the house you live in or where you photograph yourself on vacation, I think we tell ourselves we're working hard for our family to provide them with these nice things," she told me. "But for many of us, it's rooted in moving through trauma, feeling the pressure of societal influence, or comporting yourself to be accepted in certain workplaces."

Indeed, today's world perpetuates a culture of "never enough" that extends beyond the workplace and into our hands. Social media enables us to benchmark our worth against anyone and everyone. Now, The Joneses are as much The Kardashians as your neighbors down the block. All our brains need is this filter to conflate achievement with materialism. What results is envy, a hidden poison we all sip from time to time. Indulging on occasion won't destroy you, but when you imbibe too often, you begin to treat what others have and do as a reflection back onto you. What an ugly way to feel, and what a great landscape for mistakes.

Overspending is a common manifestation of the "never enough" mindset. Paige Pritchard, founder of Overcoming Overspending, a financial wellness community that helps people spend with more intention, shared with me two warning signs that spending could be a habitual problem in you or your partner's life.

The most obvious red flag is spending more than you have. If you carry a revolving credit card balance that ticks up from month-to-month, take a closer look at which of those expenses are discretionary. Ask each other how you'd feel about reducing them. If the thought of slicing your shopping budget puts you in a cold sweat even though your cash flow literally can't support what you spend, yup. You're a Never Enougher. But to be clear, even high-earning couples without credit card debt can suffer from the same affliction. You don't need to be in debt to be constantly derailing your goals.

It's a slippery slope, because the barriers to consume have never been lower. Just like easy access to student loans enabled

11. THE THIRSTIEST

the steep costs of higher education, the financial services and tech industries make it easier to borrow; to buy now and pay later; to complete frictionless payments with your thumb and your face. It's become too easy to chase lifestyles you think you deserve.

Dr. Anna Lembke, psychiatrist and author of *Dopamine Nation: Finding Balance in the Age of Indulgence*, has done extensive work around the pleasure-pain balance and continues to treat individuals who struggle to know their *enough*. As she notes, our consumer culture isn't helping. "We are surrounded by invitations to buy... accompanied by explicit and implicit messages that tell us we will be happy only after we have purchased a certain commodity," she said in an email to me. "AI-driven digital media allows for targeted and potent promotional content based on past behaviors, which in turn, triggers dopamine in an endless cycle of craving that is difficult to escape from."

From a behavioral standpoint, she said, patterns of overspending look no different than gambling, drugs, or alcohol abuse: they all require more and more dopamine over time for you to feel good or stop feeling bad. Part of the desire is the pursuit itself.

"People look for that perfect handbag, car, or pair of shoes, the one that is going to solve all our cravings, only to find that having bought it, the cravings begin again almost immediately," she said. "Like gambling addiction, shopping addiction is often accompanied by a dissociative state that suspends rational thought, and that state is the true drug, rather than the purchased object itself."

While there are societal and physiological reasons people get caught in these loops, you can't discount the personal ones, either. Oftentimes, when someone indicates they don't have enough, they are really thinking, *I am not enough*.

What they seek is just filler—sauce in a pie that's missing the fruit. Stuffing your life with material possessions, professional clout, and the perpetual sludge of envy will not fill you up. Your chase of choice matters not. These are symptoms of the same disease.

It's hard to call yourself someone who can't be satisfied. What we observed in the couples we spoke with came more from subtext than what anyone would admit. Quickly, we realized that we were missing answers to a very important question:

Do you have enough?

"You mean, money?" they'd say. "Do we think we have enough money?"

"I mean whatever *enough* means to you," I'd say. "But answer separately, please."

Some couples qualified their answers, like, *we certainly could use more money and would like to be able to retire someday, but we're happy and healthy, so sure. It's enough.*

Others shocked each other, one person saying yes; the other, absolutely not. Some replied with a version of, *it will be enough when we move houses, it will be enough when we can vacation twice a year*, but we all know how moving the goal post works.

What an incredible concept: to believe you have enough.

Throughout these pages, you will see that there are some things money can't buy. Our interviews revealed early on that the most emotionally charged financial issues between couples aren't affixed to certain numbers or benchmarks—there *is no* magic number. Beyond your ability to house, feed, and protect your family, finding peace around what you have in your life is a subjective pursuit. What feels like "enough" for you might not even come close for your partner.

What feels like "enough" might not come from money at all.

Thakor, who wrote a whole book on finding your *enough*, summarized the significance of the question perfectly. "I think about it as a scaled measure of contentment—not happiness, not joy, because we don't feel that all the time," she told me. "But contentment in the way in which you flow through the world."

She experienced firsthand what can happen when two partners aren't examining their answers to this question together. Thakor's ex-husband, who is 20 years older than her, had a successful career by the time they met. In his fifties and sixties, he was watching his senior mentors die and wanted to experience more joy in his own life.

"I rode on the back of his motorcycle through 36 countries," she told me. "But while he was enjoying the experience, I had my earbuds in listening to business books the whole time."

He felt like he had enough. She didn't.

"We were so far apart," she admitted. "I think it can irreparably ruin a marriage if you don't listen to the heartfelt rationale behind your partner's definition of *enough*."

When you're drinking from different sized glasses, you're quenching different thirsts. For reasons we examined in *Beginnings* and will dive deeper into later, many couples will find that they, as partners, want different things. That's not all bad; in fact, it could be helpful, especially when you can lean on each other's financial, emotional, and even physical support to reach your own goals. But you'll have to work to convert your actual resources into a life that satisfies you both.

Dr. Maggie Vaughan, a licensed marriage and family therapist and relationship specialist, acknowledged, "You probably didn't choose a partner who's just unreasonable or irrational. They want what they want for a reason." With empathy, "you're much more invested in building a bridge between the two positions."

Ask the question and listen to the answer. You may hear everything you need. That, or you'll realize you've just begun to learn what your partner really wants.

If you or your partner have a "never-enough" mindset, there's a very real risk that your relationship becomes no longer enough. This can be a natural progression for someone who measures their quality of life against what other people have, or who can't figure out what they're looking for, because they're not yet able to answer the hard questions about themselves.

"Is this really what you think makes you a valuable human being?" Dr. Vaughan asks, rhetorically. We'd all answer "no," but saying and believing are two different things.

How much of your own *enough* are you holding your partner responsible for? And is that fair, if they don't need as much as you to be happy?

Too often, our partners become our last line of defense. They are the closest person you can project upon before you're finally forced to turn the mirror around on yourself.

Professor Jenny Olson and I commiserated on this point, as we're all swimming against the tide of today's social pressure. The internet has us cobbling together this Frankenstein of a perfect partner—of a perfect *human*—who doesn't exist. In earlier times, people got married to survive. Now, we expect much more.

"They're not only supposed to help provide," she said. "They're supposed to help me be a better version of myself. They're supposed to be my travel partner, my cooking partner, all of these things. We just expect so much out of our partners, including financially, that it can be often difficult to reach them."

It takes a lot to admit you're never satisfied, and even more to admit why. But no matter how it manifests in your relationship, tasking your partner to support your perpetual quest for *more* isn't sustainable forever. People get tired of moving targets, especially when you've made them into one.

You are not wrong for wanting a large glass—a full one, at that. So much of this world tells us to want everything, but you could end up sorry for not knowing when you're quenched.

You may realize that *enough* meant something different than you once thought, or that *enough* happened long ago. You may realize that *enough* comes from people, not titles or things. I just hope you find it and savor every drop.

12.
WISHFUL THINKING

You can lose a lot more than money looking for hope in the wrong places.

Consider this my dirty secret: I am fascinated by cults. I will consume as much as I can about them, force Douglas into watching documentaries about them—you name it, I've seen it. I am particularly shocked by the ways modern-day cults weaponize technology to gain control over their members. They hide behind dances on TikTok; recruit through Facebook live streams; and demand blackmailing digital photos as collateral, to name just a few spurious practices. I write this at the risk of you thinking I'm entertained rather than horrified. But I guess, the issue that keeps plaguing me is: What draws people in? What makes them believe?

More relevant than what a cult believes is how they get people to believe it. Solicitation, relatability, buy-in, sacrifice, and control underpin systems that aren't limited to religious groups. We create god-like figures everywhere. Way more than we should.

The term cult can mean, "a great devotion to a person, idea, object, movement, or work."[30] Great devotion can lead a person to extremes, discarding logic in favor of something they want to believe is true no matter what.

You can learn a lot from understanding how an average person falls into the fringe. Usually, they are searching for *something*: to find direction, to get rich, to believe, to belong. Once they're sold on a pathway to having what it is they're looking for, they're willing to bet the farm—their investments, their livelihoods, their relationships—for that utopic dream.

You have to question not only the motivations behind the group selling them the dream but also why people are so susceptible. How did they ripen for the taking?

I can share a glimpse into my own brain during my tough first years out of law school. You already know about the student loan debt, but it's important to contextualize my feelings within the greater sentiment of millennials following the Great Recession.

The Occupy Wall Street movement was a swell of anger not just at big banks but at everyone. As we grew up, millennials were taught the way it would go: put your head down, work hard, go to school, things work out. Heart mattered. People mattered. Doing a good job mattered. But when it came down to it, we saw a much bleaker future unfolding right before us. Now, I wasn't about to join a campout in Zuccotti Park or anything, but truth was, I didn't know who or what to believe in anymore.

When Douglas's brilliant childhood friend called to ask if we would give him $3,000 to split the cost of a special computer that would solve a complicated math problem and reward us with a digital currency called Bitcoin, my answer wasn't what they expected. We barely had the cash in hand, and frankly, even considering it was very out of character for me. But I was done

12. WISHFUL THINKING

being told what to do. Crypto ignited a small spark of possibility at a time for me when almost nothing seemed possible. I wanted—I *needed*—that magic.

A little bit of dreaming did not disrupt our lives. We mined Bitcoin. We still believe in the possibilities of cryptocurrency and blockchain technology. We participated, but we never sold ourselves to the extreme ends of thinking about it, because we know that nothing is a one-sized-fits-all solution to our financial goals. But then again, we're not everyone.

Money cults thrive when people overlook facts for magic. Going all in on a financial concept or movement at the expense of your family's financial security could be a mistake with devastating consequences.

Lots of people get in too deep on crypto. Some of these maximalists, or "maxis," as they're called, don't believe in traditional financial systems anymore. Some people who haven't gone in quite that far still buy into crypto with blinders on.

Anna Mouland, CEO and Co-Founder of Bequest.com, summarized to us that half of crypto and blockchain developers are working on valuable, but boring, solutions to super technical issues. The other half are caught up in the internet glitz, pumping meme coins and building communities that draw you into ideas that may not be substantiated.

One quick search of the X account @coinfessions will show you the people who lost their spouse's money, their parent's money, or their own savings getting "rugged" (that is, having the rug pulled from underneath them) because they believed too hard. They didn't ask enough questions, because money cults breed environments where you *cannot* question. In many such communities, if you express skepticism about their business plans or the functions of what they're trying to do, they'll label you a hater and banish you from the group. Have blind faith or go back to your evil paper money. If it sounds extreme, that's because it is.

People get sold into extreme wishful thinking because they are trying to solve big problems in their lives and aren't sure how. Big problems such as: not feeling worthy; not feeling successful; not feeling loved; or not feeling like you're adding value to your partnership.

Crypto maxis are just one example of how people can be groomed into wishing for life-changing miracles. Long before anyone could decentralize their money, others were stacking theirs into pyramids. I'll explain.

Some companies recruit people to sell directly to consumers using multi-level marketing. "MLM" companies encourage their independent distributors to both promote and sell their products *and* recruit new salespeople into the business model. The recruited become distributors themselves, who then earn a percentage of sales off the new recruits downstream from them.[31] And down and down it goes.

To be clear, not all MLM operations are illegal pyramid schemes. In the Seventies, after the Federal Trade Commission accused Amway (short for "American Way"), which was perhaps the first and most prevalent MLM company, of a host of serious accusations, the court held that Amway had changes to make, but they ultimately prevailed. The Commission's landmark decision outlined the differences between a legitimate MLM operation and an illegal pyramid scheme, providing a framework for MLMs to flourish within the boundaries of the law for years to come.[32] I'll take a page from my ethics training and say that just because something's legal doesn't make it right. In the shadows of a private living room or text conversation, people can noodle around a lot.

Now, the global direct-selling market is projected to reach more than $219 billion, with more than 7.3 million direct sellers in the United States.[33] Around 75% of MLM participants are women,[34] which tells you something about who's sliding into the DMs with a "Hey, Hun!" the most.

12. WISHFUL THINKING

Just as the state of the banking system contributed to the rise of crypto, American conservatism contributed to the rise of MLMs, presenting the idea that women can fulfill their proclaimed responsibilities as a wife and mother while earning extra income for their households. MLMs claim to offer a simple solution for a complex problem as the worldwide cost of living skyrocketed, making life on one salary no longer tenable for most families. Prospective members often have less financial education and are making ends meet in working-class jobs, so the opportunity to earn an extra paycheck is more than a gift. It is a prayer answered.

"People feel like they've exhausted every single option, and the only thing left is this one crazy thing," said Roberta Blevins, who educates people on the dangerous culture of MLMs through TikTok and her podcast, "Life After MLM." She was also featured in *LulaRich*, a docuseries chronicling the tribulations of LulaRoe, an infamous womenswear MLM business known for its supersoft leggings (even I owned a few pairs). When Blevins told me an MLM business "can be whatever you want it to be," I didn't grasp the extent of it, until she explained.

The grooming begins before you even join, she said. You see these well-manicured women giggling together, having fun, vacationing on lavish trips, all thanks to [insert MLM here]. FOMO is the bait into private conversations, where recruiters tailor their messages based on personal information they learn about you: your family, your pain points, your desires. In any case, the MLM is your solution. *Need another $200 per month?* They'll help you earn it. *Want to be your own girl boss?* You can. *Looking for mom friends?* You will find your best friends. *Hoping to save your marriage?* Your husband will respect the woman you can be. Whatever the holes in your life are, the MLM will fill them. Whatever the product, it will allegedly "sell itself."

"It really is this idea of dreaming, and then dreaming beyond that dream, and then dreaming just beyond that dream," she said.

Blevins didn't take the decision to become a LulaRoe distributor lightly. She and her then-husband mulled it over for weeks. Blevins used to be the breadwinner before having kids and leaving the workforce to raise them, but when she wasn't earning an income, she felt a shift. He put an alert on their credit card for when she spent more than $100, which understandably felt controlling to her. For a "little spending cash," as he said, she started hustling with side jobs like baking cupcakes for friends and working as a hair stylist in Los Angeles in the later hours after he got home from work. "I would take that spending cash as my freedom, because I wasn't getting it anywhere else."

Blevins took out a business line of credit with her bank to make her initial $9,000 investment into inventory. And on paper, she was successful. During her 18-month tenure with LulaRoe, she received monthly bonus checks, maintained profitability, and grew her team to almost 75 salespeople under her. But any notion that she "had it all" was wrong.

She worked 24/7 to earn *maybe* equal to what she made working part-time at the salon. Her recruits, whom she'd grown close to, started to either leave or consider taking measures to stay afloat that didn't sit well with her. One team member was two months behind on her mortgage and considered doubling her investment into buying the new collection. Blevins stopped her. Corporate did nothing to address quality concerns, leaving its "business owners" to fend for themselves with solutions like putting leggings that reeked of mildew into the freezer.

"I started thinking to myself, I don't think this is a business."

When she left LulaRoe, she was excommunicated. Everything was gone: the friendships, the connections, the good it did for her relationship. In some respects, she told me, LulaRoe did help her marriage when her husband showed he was proud of her. "In those moments, I was like, my God, it's saving our marriage," she confessed. "But again, once you leave something, everything goes with it. So that connection we had with that was done."

12. WISHFUL THINKING

They divorced several years after she left LulaRoe. MLM wasn't the reason, but the problems she thought it would solve were. **It doesn't matter if leggings, digital coins, or anything else is for sale. What matters is what you're seeking and why you're not receiving it already.**

When you or the person you love start looking for miracles to fill those needs, you end up in the wrong places with people who can take advantage of you.

If something seems too good to be true, it is. Nothing is more obvious than that, but when you're in a vulnerable state, it's much easier to abandon your critical reasoning skills, because you *want* it to be true. If you or your partner are feeling hopeless or out of options, you're there. You're susceptible. Be skeptical.

When you are moving deeper into an online community, or school of thought, or business opportunity, ask yourself these questions:

- Are they telling you something in private that they can't tell you in public?
- Are they addressing your legitimate concerns or just labeling you a non-believer?
- Are they suggesting you distance yourself from people you love, because they couldn't possibly understand the work of the community?
- Are they consistently asking you to double-down on your time, money, or commitment?

If you can answer *yes* to any or all of this, you're dealing with a group that wants something you shouldn't give them.

Everyone loves to wish. Some of us need our wishes to come true more than others. But wishes without facts are just magic, and your needs can't be met with that.

13. WHAT HAPPENS NEXT

This is the chapter about lying.

Almost forty percent of U.S. adults who are married or cohabitating with a partner admit they've held financial secrets.[35] The damage can be significant: almost the same percentage of adults who uncover this type of dishonesty would consider calling quits on their relationship.[36]

It's important to define financial infidelity, because in real life, not every omission rises to a level worth calling your partner's trust into question. Saying, *no babe, I didn't go to Target today*, probably isn't so bad. But even lots of little lies can become A Big Lie when you let your standards slip away.

Professor Jenny Olson and her colleagues set forth a two-part definition for financial infidelity that I really appreciate: "(1) engaging in a financial behavior expected to elicit disapproval from one's partner and (2) intentionally failing to disclose this behavior to one's partner."[37] Making serious hidden purchases, hiding debts and bank accounts, and even lying about your income, are some

13. WHAT HAPPENS NEXT

of the ways people lie about money to their partners. But intent really seals the deal here.

Throughout this entire section, we've been exploring financial decisions that people regret, to varying degrees and outcomes. But those decisions were visible. However you or your partner felt about them, at least you knew the facts.

Hiding them is a purposeful act. A secondary offense. A cut deeper than money.

Julia remembers opening the mail: "FINAL NOTICE," it read. She never saw the earlier ones.

She had thought they were getting by and making it work. Years before, she and her husband Brandon suffered a series of devastating miscarriages that left them in a pile of grief and medical bills. But their two healthy daughters arrived, forming the family she had wanted since the time she took Brandon home from college to meet her Southern Baptist parents.

"He was a nice guy who loved Jesus, and that checked all the boxes," she said, looking back on the naïveté of her youth. "I couldn't have even articulated what I wanted—what I *actually* wanted, because I didn't know."

Brandon hopped from job to job, never with much of a plan. It was always something. When he went back to school, Julia just hoped he would emerge a provider, a role she was taught belonged to husbands. But the way she worked—coaching at the gym, selling nutritional products, doing whatever she could to make a few hundred bucks—makes me believe she knew it wasn't true.

The final notice was for the $19,000 balance on a credit card Brandon had opened in both of their names. That wasn't the only one. In total, they owed about $30,000 in debt she didn't know about, on top of the medical debt she did. In all the pain she experienced with loss, this was somehow worse.

"Part of my rage was that he knew this was going on," she

explained. "Why wasn't he doing more to solve it? Why was he just crawling under a rock?"

I asked Dr. Victoria Elf Raymond, who you heard from earlier in this section, why people lie. She said, plainly, "because they don't want to get caught."

It was a moment of levity on a tough topic. Most people, she said, feel horrible when they lie and cheat. When money's involved, their actions may have even come from a good place, but something went wrong, so they lied to avoid a fight. The lie compounds and compounds. It can take on a life of its own. She said that in a sense, some people are relieved when they get caught.

I know why people lie. Because they are weak. Broken. Self-sabotaging. Because they believe they don't deserve better than the situation they've created. People lie to avoid reality. People lie when they can't see a way out.

Julia's husband never really explained why. She pleaded with him for answers, but he would just shut down. She sent him to crash with a friend for a bit, but her fixes were Band-Aids, not solutions. They borrowed money from family to pay off enough of the debt to feel stable. She took over the bills. They moved to a city for him to start fresh after graduate school, but a year later, things felt just like before.

Brandon lost both of his jobs in one day. He told her this much, but then he also let her know about the personal line of credit he took out at a new bank.

"The first time just made me angry," she admitted. "The second time, I was just like, okay, maybe he's never going to figure it out. Maybe he's never going to take care of our family. Maybe I have to figure this out and do that for us, because something in him must be broken."

Earlier in *Mistakes*, I shared an example from my own life of what can result when you shame yourself for your financial

13. WHAT HAPPENS NEXT

decisions. Dr. Maggie Vaughan spoke to me about the dual effect of shame in a partnership.

"Shaming your partner has a major impact," she said. "The question is whether it will have the impact you want it to have."

Shaming your partner will make them feel bad about themselves, which, sure, might be well deserved. But what they do with your shame might not be constructive. You'd hope it would cause them to change, but as Dr. Vaughan explained, it could also shift the power dynamic to more of a parent-child relationship, where resentment and anger build.

When you know you're going to be shamed, that's also more reason to keep lying.

Julia changed careers to financially support them all. The learning curve was steep, her hours long at work and at home. But she built that career. I had hoped she felt a spark of possibility in herself amongst her disappointment in her husband. But she told me, her motivation was 80% fear and 20% ambition. Not quite the silver lining I wanted for her.

For years, she didn't really care what Brandon was doing. He bopped from job to job until working under a friend at his family therapy practice. But when Brandon brought her the terms of a legal agreement for him to start a new practice together with that friend, the deal seemed off. It was too one-sided. Almost punitive.

Julia took matters into her own hands and called their friend. Brandon had failed to report $13,000 in shared business revenue with him. He was either signing this deal or getting sued.

"I don't know how late we stayed up that night. I don't know how many questions I asked," she said.

There was more. He had yet another hidden bank account where he put his money to spend it on whatever he wanted, outside of the household finances that Julia managed. She didn't find out that night. It took several more weeks for him to come clean.

"I remember thinking at the time, there's no amount of remorse that could satisfy me. I didn't care if he was remorseful. I wasn't interested in his feelings any longer," she explained. "It caused such a deep level of distrust that it's intimacy breaking."

There's a principle in law called *res ipsa loquitur*. It means, "the thing speaks for itself." In other words, the facts are so obviously bad that you don't need to know much else.

When we began research for this book, I set a rule that we would only tell a story if we could speak with all parties involved. Unless one of them was divorced, sick, or dead, I needed them both. But here, I only got to interview Julia. They weren't divorced, but they weren't exactly together, either. Right after our conversation, I kicked myself for not insisting I speak with Brandon. I thought about going back, about what I would say. But in time, I realized, it didn't matter. There are no rules in how I do this.

He did what he did, and he did it enough that I stopped caring why. The piece of the story that mattered to me was hers. Would she keep writing it, or was it already over?

After the drama with his friend's business, Julia separated from Brandon. He signed a one-year apartment lease to give them both space.

They went to therapy to try to unpack all that happened over the years. He didn't want to get divorced and asked why she was giving up on him now. She told him: "The only way for me to reestablish peace is to remove myself from the chaos that you are."

Beneath any lies that damage your relationship, there is either a deep sense of connection you are both still grasping onto, or there is not. You either both want to rebuild, or you do not.

Dr. Vaughan and Dr. Raymond each told me that trust and forgiveness require both parties to want to do the work. Sometimes, people agree to couples therapy because they feel guilty, or they don't like the concept of divorce. But if they are not demonstrating a willingness to learn why they did it or change their behavior, then it's hard to hope things will improve.

13. WHAT HAPPENS NEXT

Rebuilding trust requires radical transparency. When you beg someone to trust you again, you're standing on nothing, explained Dr. Vaughan. Transparency is all you can give them, so you should give them all of it they need.

Sometimes, it's just not enough.

I asked Dr. Raymond when it's time to walk away. She said, when you're evolving and they're standing still.

Brandon ended up moving back in. Their separation was having a significant impact on their teenage daughter's mental health, and Julia felt that none of her own needs were more important than that.

"We have nothing else in common right now," she said. "So, we both agree our role in life right now is creating health and safety for the kids."

It's not my place to write the end of their story; to say when it ends or how. Besides, I don't know what to want for Julia, other than the best.

Love is a standard. You can meet it or expand it. You can bend it or damage it until it's no longer recognizable.

But underneath whatever you make of your standards, there is a bright-lined rule. You will both fight for your love if you want it. You will not walk away because people think you should, or because you're afraid, or because things have gotten more complicated. And when one of you stops fighting, you will recognize it. You will acknowledge it. And you will decide what happens next.

YOUR QUESTIONS ON MISTAKES

1. What is your biggest money regret?
2. How does it still impact your life today?
3. Are you confident in managing your money?
4. What is one thing you'd change about how you handle money together?
5. What is one thing you do well together?
6. Do you have enough?
7. If you don't, what would make you feel like you did?
8. Have you ever sold yourself on something you wanted to be true?
9. Have you ever made a financial decision your partner would disagree with... and do they know about it?

PART III.
CONTRIBUTIONS

You're in the heart of it now. Think about the people you're reading this for: your partner, your children, your loved ones, yourself. When it comes to your closest relationships, money's just one of the currencies that matter. Time is a currency, too.

We are about to expand your idea of what it means to contribute. This is the biggest reframe you can learn from us. As a society, our lens is too tight, too focused on who *produces* and not enough on how we *provide*. When you contribute, you care, teach, enable, and support. You show up in the best and worst of times. Contributing doesn't look the same for everyone, but you should both feel proud of the ways you do it, and you should both believe it's fair.

Money and care are inextricably linked. That truth comes on quick as new parents. You'll learn that life moves in seasons, decisions are fluid, and the challenges will keep on coming. The impact of caregiving can reach beyond your finances and into your career, self-worth, and identity. Caregivers lose their seat at many tables in many ways, only some of which are on purpose. Sometimes, the clouds roll in, and we just have to weather the storm.

But when you're finished with this section, you will see the invisible. One partner's time isn't worth more than the other's. In a relationship, you both have roles to play. We will dive deep into the physical, mental, and financial sides of labor, because all work is important. Leveling the scale of labor gives an overworked spouse back their time so they can reinvest in themselves and find their seats at whatever tables they want.

Just know, this will not be all diapers and a Sisyphean mountain of socks. There are other costs of caring for those we love. We will show you the emotional toll of fractured systems that don't allow our loved ones to age and die with grace. You will be assured of the strength you have inside and reminded of what matters most.

14. WYKYK (WHEN YOU KNOW, YOU KNOW)

Becoming parents will rock your world. In this season of life, the math may not math.

I'm sure you know the term, *fake it 'til you make it*. I can't stand it, to be honest. Maybe because it reminds me of a time when I thought I had to know everything. Put on an armor of confidence at work so your bosses won't see you sweat. Keep it on for your friends and family so they won't see you falter.

This is flawed thinking, because nobody knows everything. You don't need to. You just need to understand what you know and what you don't.

Never did we know less about anything than when we became parents. You can't know about parenting until you're doing it—and even then, you only know what you know.

Our oldest daughter, Hazel, was born five weeks early after my water broke all over our bathroom floor, like it does in the movies. Things were already not going as planned. Two nights later, the hospital discharged us onto the cold, noisy avenue without a moment for photos to spare. We hurried our new baby into my mom's car circling the block and crawled in the bus lane back to our New York City apartment.

Nothing felt right. Her nursery—a dining nook off the kitchen—was stacked with unpacked boxes, an unmade crib, and unwashed clothes, all too big for a four-and-a-half-pound preemie. She was too small, the moment too big. We planned to live in the city for a long time, but from the minute we brought her home, my heart looked for a way out of there. Having a baby changed everything.

You don't know, until you know.

Before having kids, you might live for years within predictable routines and rituals: who pays the bills; when you hit the gym; how often you go for a date night; which friends you watch football with every weekend. You can try your best to cling to these certainties after kids, but chances are, they won't all stick. Your lives become as fluid as sleep schedules and tiny teeth popping through.

Children will cause a seismic shift in how you think about your time, your money, and the ways you need each other. It's uncomfortable as hell, and not just because you're tired—*tired* isn't even the half of it.

Research now shows that during matrescence, a term for the transition into motherhood, women experience physiological, biological, hormonal, physical, and emotional changes. I asked Dr. Nicole Pensak, clinical psychologist and author of *Rattled: How to Calm New Mom Anxiety with the Power of the Postpartum Brain*, to oversimplify it for anyone trying to understand what their partner's going through. And she did:

"Your partner's becoming a completely different person from the inside out," she said. "It's about to rock your world."

14. WYKYK (WHEN YOU KNOW, YOU KNOW)

Dr. Pensak explained that while the physiological changes come on quick after having a baby, the psychological side takes time to catch up, leaving some new mothers, well, rattled.

Up to 85% of new mothers experience the "baby blues," or a temporary state of sadness. But postpartum depression impacts 10-15 % of White women and even higher percentages of women from other racial and ethnic backgrounds. They all may experience intense feelings of despair, anxiety, fear, guilt, and exhaustion that begin in the year following childbirth and can last up to several years. When a mother struggles, her partner is more likely to struggle. Ten percent of new dads also suffer from depression or anxiety, because they're experiencing deep emotional changes, too.[38]

One mom I spoke with, Cassie, had a great perspective on this. In her teaching career, she always received such positive reinforcement from her colleagues, administrators, parents, and even her students. But those short feedback loops don't exist with babies. "When I was home with two babies who don't speak, there was no one to let me know I was doing a good job," she said. "They weren't telling me, 'Mom, you're doing great today.' That was hard for me."

Sure, her husband should have been telling her she was doing a good job. They'll acknowledge it. I'll acknowledge it, too. But without postpartum resources in place—for mom and dad—you might just be in triage mode, drinking from the hose.

Dr. Pensak's seen relationship satisfaction plummet in the early years of parenting, which shouldn't surprise any parents anywhere. No one's needs are being met except for The Baby. The Baby is the seventh wonder of your world. The Baby is also terrifying. The Baby is a living, breathing question with very few answers.

Decisions feel heavy, and early on, there are just too many of them to make. With Hazel, I'd spend hours excavating the internet for the pros and cons of every single sleep sack, worrying my choice could mean life or death. Like a tick, the horror stories burrowed into my postpartum brain. Logic and reason were present but slightly out of reach.

In the moment, it's hard to keep your chin up. But something wonderful takes place as you rise to these relentless challenges. You are problem solving at a pace you've never run before. Dr. Pensak explained that mothers build new neural networks in their postpartum period. With each pivot, we stretch the plasticity of our brains.

We are developing, too.

Parenting calls on you to be flexible—with your time and your money. Harder than any sleep regression is accepting the fact that your children's needs will constantly change, and so will yours. You are new people, who only know what you know.

As parents, you need to let go of your preconceived notions when your present-day feelings are at odds with them. Clinging too hard to the rigid plans or strategies you put in place before children won't help you identify what everyone actually needs.

Tara and Scott were off to a rough start. They had talked about having kids—in a loose, conceptual sense—but in the middle of the night, Scott heard Tara rustling around in the bathroom and knew.

"Pregnant?" he asked.

"Yup," she said.

And then, he began to spiral.

"Money came to my mind immediately," he said. "I was grilling her for the rest of the night." They laid awake, him peppering her with questions about the costs of daycare, the costs of everything, whether Tara should go back to work or stay home. He wanted answers right then and there; answers she couldn't give, of course.

His reaction wasn't great, but let's not get down on Scott too much. The bombshell of Tara's pregnancy triggered an earthquake to his internal security. Scott wasn't wrong for having a million and one questions—when you're panicked sometimes, it's hard to stop

14. WYKYK (WHEN YOU KNOW, YOU KNOW)

yourself. He handles the family's finances and felt an overwhelming sense of responsibility over the initial decisions they'd have to make. At one point, he told me, he wasn't ready. But "ready" is not a benchmark worth striving for in this context.

To anyone who feels they aren't ready, I'd ask in return, not ready for what? The care, the cost, the love, or never knowing what comes next?

They had twins, by the way.

I keep returning to this one memory from our foggy days of new parenthood. The walls in our city apartment were thick cement—terrible for a baby monitor—and our bedroom was down a narrow hall from the dining nook where Hazel slept. In the depths of my own anxiety, she felt miles away. So, for a few weeks, Douglas and I decided to sleep on the pullout couch to be closer to her during feeds in the middle of the night. We did all of them together. Both of us. The experts would call us insane for not taking turns, but for that time, it was what we needed.

Not all decisions you make for your family win on paper. That doesn't mean they're wrong.

When it comes to money, having children blurs the line of what makes sense. Your finances won't always drive what's in their best interests or what you as parents need to feel secure as caregivers.

In other words, your family is not a logistic. They're not a strategy. The math may not math.

Tara and Scott found this out for themselves. Before having the twins, they bought a townhome next door to a wannabe fitness guru. Every morning at 4 a.m., they'd hear him clinking around and slamming weights on the floor. And every night, they'd hear him screaming in the most belligerent fights with his spouse. It was one thing before the babies arrived, but the hostile environment bleeding through their shared wall was bleeding into their lives. This was in 2021, when Florida home prices skyrocketed because of the pandemic and many workers, including Scott, were working from home. He was making a bit more money than during Tara's pregnancy, but as he put it, "not enough to buy a house that was two-and-a-half times the last one we bought."

The math didn't math, but they moved, anyway.

To be clear, you can't allow your baby-pink-colored glasses to completely distort reality. Cathy Curtis, CFP®, cautions new parents against overextending themselves during the nesting process. Housing costs can be insane, and people tend to underestimate the annual costs to maintain a home and property.

I'm sure another financial advisor, like Curtis, would have told us not to buy our home in the suburbs when we did. Poor Douglas stretched himself far out of his comfort zone to accommodate my visceral need to get our baby the hell out of New York City. We used almost all our cash savings to close, buy a couch, and handle a few tiny touch-ups. We don't regret it, by any means. But I do look back and think about how many assumptions we made and how few answers we had before jumping headfirst into our most significant joint financial decision ever. The math wouldn't have changed much, but had we waited a little longer, we could've acted with a little less emotion and a little more intention around what we purchased. Maybe we could've had a garage.

When parenting, though, you will never be able to reconcile every single choice with every single feeling you both have about the situation. By trying, you will drive each other crazy or be paralyzed by indecision. We take leaps of faith with our kids every day. We are not irresponsible for it. We're just doing the best we can do.

Instead of searching too hard for clarity, embrace that many truths can exist at once.

I learned in high school that the word "and" is the most important tool in improvisational theater. The word "and" accepts what you just heard and builds upon it. The word "and" expands the story.

14. WYKYK (WHEN YOU KNOW, YOU KNOW)

In her book, Dr. Pensak used the word "and" to describe the complexities that children bring into our lives, because yes, they are wonderful *and* scary. They are too expensive *and* our favorite people to spend money on. They make us miss our time alone *and* love each other more. They galvanize our priorities *and* have us question everything.

Looking back, my conversation with Curtis also revealed two truths: you can't let emotions drive you to overextend yourselves beyond reason, *and* you can know these most jarring, expensive early years of parenting are not forever.

"Don't just focus on the next ten years," she tells her clients. "You're young, you're able, you have career skills, you're worth so much. Trust yourselves." Expand your story *and* make room for context. "It can be very fluid if you keep your minds open."

For parents, seasons are no longer just weather. Your lives now move in seasons. High-touch seasons. All-hands-on-deck seasons. Birthday seasons. Seasons between schoolyears. Seasons between caregivers. Seasons that feel so perfect you wish to stop time.

But you can't stop time. You're always in motion.

15. CAREGIVERS ARE PROVIDERS

You contribute to your family in more ways than earning money.

My classmate bestowed the honor of speaking at our law school graduation wasn't the student body president, or frankly, one of my peers at all. She was a seasoned mother with a message: you can't have it all.

I remember it so well, because that's when I stopped listening to her.

(Men reading this book: don't check out like I did. You need this chapter as much as we do.)

Intelligent women filled the seats around me, all taught from a young age that we *could*. The numbers supported it then, and even more so now, with women earning the majority of higher education degrees in the United States.[39] Our eyes don't deceive us. College-educated women have now surpassed the number of college-educated men in the workforce.[40] Even back in the 2010s, we embodied that progress, trading our once suggested courtroom

15. CAREGIVERS ARE PROVIDERS

attire (pencil skirts) for pantsuits. We didn't need the banality of a social media movement to feel our potential. Beyoncé told us we'd run the world, and we believed it.

But I wish I had paid attention. The woman standing before us had moved through many seasons of her life, raising many children, playing many roles. There was a time for them and a time for her. What she did was a triumph, even though her message flew in the face of every lesson I had ever learned about female ambition. For all of us, I didn't want to believe that anything—or anyone—would stand in our way.

Something happens to women in the timeframe between taking up half of the office cubicles and so few corner offices. Blaming the symbolic glass ceiling gets trickier when more women than ever are busting through it, but a noticeable gap does exist across the labor force. According to LeanIn.Org's Women in the Workplace report, women assume just 34% of positions at the Vice President level and just 29% in the C-Suite. We are climbing ladders with broken rungs, missing opportunities for those first promotions: the ones that build momentum in our careers and give us access to the high-level roles.[41]

It's not a coincidence that many of us have children during that same window of time. Suddenly, a track that seemed predestined has detours, pitstops, and forks in the road. Some of them we choose. Others are chosen for us. Some, we aren't quite sure whether they chose or we did.

Brittney, for example, felt it all. She quit two jobs and lost a third trying to care for her young daughter, whose challenges had not yet revealed the formal diagnosis later deemed autism spectrum disorder and ADHD. During the pandemic, she had no choice but to homeschool her for three years to make sure she got the support she needed. Her daughter's back to school now with better resources, but Brittney still bears the lion's share of responsibility for her, given her husband Charles's demanding job.

"I wish it was different, but it's not," she said. "One of us has to be that person, you know? Like we both can't be in full-time work right now or we would all die."

The Bermuda Triangle of my career lasted five years. I faced adversity following the births of both of my daughters, not only in missed opportunities but in colleagues' perception of me. What I could live up to. What I would tolerate. How quickly I could be diminished out of relevance. When the ground begins to shake under your feet, it can feel like a stunning betrayal. Pairing such an emotional reality check with the actual challenges of caregiving young children, any mother has a right to question her place.

Don't internalize the way our systems fail parents as personal failures of your own.

In America, we don't just set mothers up to fail. We make them believe they're the problem. Thankfully, mothers are mobilizing to solve these problems, like Raena Boston, co-founder of Chamber of Mothers, a policy advocacy group connecting moms with local governments. Boston didn't have paid family leave until her third child and immediately felt the difference in her mental health and her family's finances. This drove her to help other mothers find their voices and bring them to the ballots.

"If we ever want things to change, it starts with how we treat caregiving in this country," she said.

Lack of adequate paid family leave is a primary contributor to our caregiving woes. Only one in four private sector employees has access to any paid family leave, and that number is much less for the lowest 10% of earners.[42] Even after we survive those early months with a newborn, the childcare crisis persists well into grade school, and we know this a couple of ways. In a survey conducted by Care.com, parents reported spending almost a quarter of their household income on childcare. Even worse, they're using almost *a third* of their savings on childcare costs, and these figures only

15. CAREGIVERS ARE PROVIDERS

graze atop the labyrinth of childcare solutions most families need to patch together to make their lives work.[43]

It shouldn't be like this. Full stop.

Without adequate federal and state subsidies, the total cost to run childcare programs is borne by the providers and the parents, which will result in one of three outcomes: the programs lose money and become less reliable as costs rise; parents stretch themselves to pay more for the same services; or one parent leaves the workforce (and we know who that usually is).

The National Women's Law Center shared a telling conclusion about who government support for better childcare impacts the most. In states that made a significant investment into their childcare infrastructure, the share of *women* with children under 12 who *wanted* to work but weren't working for pay because they were caring for their children decreased by 15%.[44] In other words, 15% less women felt their hands forced by circumstance in those states. Imagine what the workforce—what our whole economy—would look like if more women who wanted to keep going, could.

Susan can quantify her missed opportunities. She's a lawyer who runs her own firm and gets paid on contingency (which means, when her clients get paid). She had her children in her forties and already built her reputation, but her income relied on how many cases she could manage. When their daycare center closed during the pandemic for nine months, she could barely take phone calls, let alone settle cases while caring for her small children in their 1,200-square-foot condo. They went through all their savings. The firm went into debt.

"We had this plan to move to the suburbs and buy a house by kindergarten, but then the housing prices doubled, and I didn't make any money," she told me. "I felt betrayed that the path I laid out was just pulled out from under me."

Betrayed by who, I asked. "By fate, I don't know. By the zero-interest-rate policy that blew up housing prices. But really, my daycare, for closing. My life would have been totally different had I been able to work."

Susan has the right idea. It's not one person's fault.

You didn't create today's landscape for mothers. But what you do now can make it better.

Men, dads, I know you also feel the impact of strained childcare systems, and I write this with the utmost respect: I hope you feel it. You *should* feel responsible for your children beyond providing for them financially. Employers, society, and even family members may not fully grasp the unique challenges facing this generation of caregivers. But these are not your spouse's burdens to bear alone. Here are some ways to show that:

Caregive out loud. Bring your whole life to work, the way a mother must from the minute she tells the world she's pregnant. Take all available paternity leave—no excuses. "If your partner has paid leave available to them and they are not taking it, they are perpetuating the problem," Raena Boston said. Call out sick for your children's doctor's visits. Handle pick-up. Let them wander into your Zoom screen (Douglas has the girls say hi all the time). The narrative can only change when men normalize their role as caregivers, too.

Look past the numbers. Remember from the last chapter how the math may not math? If you're deciding whether she should leave the workforce to care for your children, *do not create a false equivalency between her salary and the cost to hire outside help.* This diminishes a mother's contributions to her family and fails to account for her career growth in years to come. You can't measure her lost opportunity costs and the way she feels about herself against a stranger's hourly wage.

Just care. You should care about the mother of your children and the mothers who you work with. You should care about supporting policies that get more of us into corner offices who want that for ourselves.

15. CAREGIVERS ARE PROVIDERS

And you should honor the mothers who don't want it—not now, maybe not ever.

There's that duality of parenthood again. The dilemmas of caregiving barely hold a flame to the beauty of how our hearts grow for our kids. Living a full life includes a new kind of love: one of legacy and the continuity of our values as people. Time can feel endless given the lessons we must teach them *and* fleeting in the warmth we can provide when they are young. They will never stop needing us *and* we can't get this time back. In this chapter of life, focusing on your children is okay, too.

Should a mother wish to embrace a season of caregiving for her children, both partners have financial decisions to make that will impact their family. But first, you must rethink everything you've been taught about stay-at-home mothers. (I won't call them that again.)

Over the last many decades, we've developed a binary vision of women: we work, or we stay home. Which is strange, because women were an integral part of the workforce during World War II, but the fault lines began to form when many refused to settle back into their former domestic roles. Eventually, the media latched onto a narrative of The Career Women versus The Mommies, siphoning us into their divisive advertising demographics (Pantyhose! Crock-Pots!) and pushing us further apart. Social media has a polarizing effect on almost any debate. Mothers are meant to feel like feminists or #tradwives with little room for nuance.

Neha Ruch realized it shouldn't be like this. After ten years in digital marketing, she downshifted her career to focus on her small children. What she found in her baby's music class surprised her.

"I was sitting cross-legged on the floor with all these women who had been in finance, fashion, education, nursing, social work, a myriad of different industries, who are making similar conscious shifts," she realized. "We're ambitious and we're feminist, and it's okay. Downshifting for a chapter is not at odds with ambition—and none of this matched the stereotypical June Cleaver model of the stay-at-home mother."

She wrote *The Power Pause* after founding a community of the same name, which supports ambitious women navigating career breaks for motherhood. I first found Ruch's work during the pandemic, while working fully remote for the first time as a corporate lawyer. I had been trying to bring my whole self to my job, setting boundaries and making my children visible, but being home with them full-time (albeit while employed) reframed my whole concept of what it means to be ambitious.

Ambition isn't just for the workplace. Use your ambition to care for your children, your community, and other things that matter to you.

"If we don't redefine ambition for ourselves, someone else will redefine it for us," she said. "And if we feel we are somehow not ambitious, we count ourselves out of the conversation."

When Douglas and I spoke with couples about their *enough*, they didn't list their last four job titles. Living a full life comes from a richer bank of love and purpose.

But to be fair, leaving a job to care for your children can be more of an emotional challenge than expected. Kristie had always dreamed of staying home with her kids, but when she got pregnant, she had a good remote role that she'd been excelling at for some time. She tried to do both for a few months but felt "everyone was getting 50% of me," and left when her daughter was five months old.

Staying home was supposed to be what she always wanted.

"I think Kristie felt like she lost some of her identity," said her husband.

"My goodness, so much," she agreed. "I went from people counting on me to thinking well, my daughter's more important, so I'm going to choose her. And then all the sudden, I'm wiping butts all day."

15. CAREGIVERS ARE PROVIDERS

Looking deeper, it weighed on Kristie to no longer be making money. She had worked since she was *nine years old*:

> That's what gave me purpose: always working hard so I could save more money. And then I walked away from the paycheck to raise a baby, who didn't pay me anything. I love her so much, but it was hard for me mentally to not have a job I was trying to get better at every day, besides being a mom. It made me feel like, what's my worth?

Kristie, like so many others, was counting herself out of the conversation. She internalized a message we've been fed our whole lives—a message that limits our beliefs around what we can have and when we can have it.

The message is that people who stay home consume. People who work, provide.

Let's end that right now.

Caregivers are providers.
Caregivers are providers.
Caregivers are providers.

Regardless of whether you earn a paycheck, you are providing incredible value to your family. You are the parent who is present. The one who takes on most of the emotional labor and the household administration. You facilitate your partner's ability to earn money outside of the home. You are more than a babysitter. You provide.

This reframe can change everything about your relationship with money and each other.

Too many women we spoke with admitted feeling like they couldn't spend money because they weren't earning it anymore. Their husbands weren't always perpetuating this idea, though they weren't exactly helping, either. These feelings arose from their internal scripts tethering their self-worth exclusively to their careers, thereby devaluing their work as caregivers. Our freedom to spend is an illustration of our greater financial autonomy, and really, our perception of power. You shouldn't be giving up all of yours because you're prioritizing your children.

Caregivers need to maintain an active role in their family's finances and have equal access to household income.

"This is a joint household investment," Ruch said. You need real access—not just knowing your login and password or keeping a debit card in your wallet. "The idea of becoming a financial dependent calls into question the security of your marriage or partnership," Ruch said, but "your family is an interdependent organization." You have to treat it as such, not just with money but in setting expectations around how you divide labor, which we'll get to in the next chapter.

When one partner considers a career pause, the conversation is bigger than whether you can afford it. You need to discuss how you'll do it and how you plan to treat each other.

Be honest: can you stomach such a drastic financial and emotional change? Do you carry any stigmas around parents who work inside the home?

If you aren't sure, maybe a downshift would be better for you than a full-blown pause. Explore fractional or part-time roles that allow you to keep building independent wealth but can offer you that chance to realign your priorities.

Similar to the power dynamics shaped by marrying into money, full-time caregivers need to remain vigilant about creating space for their personal growth and development. Whether you choose to stay connected to your industry through LinkedIn or local meetups or pursue new sports or hobbies, stay an active participant in your own life. Don't hand it all over to the kids. They're adorable,

15. CAREGIVERS ARE PROVIDERS

sure, but you matter. And your partner should never diminish you into a smaller version of the person you are.

Remember, even this difficult season is a season like all the others. Whether you lean in, downshift, or pause. Whether you chose it, or it happened. You are not forever bound where you are. You have a right to be who you are today. You have a right to be someone else tomorrow.

16.
DIVIDE AND CONQUER

When you're delegating household responsibilities, fairness has everything to do with how you think about time.

In the last chapter, you learned to see through a wider lens. Caregivers are providers, no matter who earns the paychecks. How you think about caregiving honors the work.

Now, you can sort out what's fair.

If someone were to ask how you contribute to your household, what would you say?

I'm going to bet that one of you will lead with money. Maybe your income is all you'll say: *my salary supports our family.* This could be true. But if you're the one carrying the family on your back, you'll mention it all: *grocery shopping, registering for school and programs, making appointments, planning special occasions.* According to Pew Research data, women carry a heavier home life load in

16. DIVIDE AND CONQUER

almost all heterosexual marriages. The only exception is for the 16% of women who are sole breadwinners—and even there, wives and husbands are doing roughly the same.[45]

In Western cultures, we've been taught to believe that time spent earning money is more valuable than time spent on anything else. Productivity is measured in goods produced—not errands run. Capitalism is a hell of a drug to keep us thinking this way. As a result, we embody harmful messages about who deserves things, not only out in the world but just as importantly, in our homes. These messages impact how we ascribe responsibilities to care for one another, creating lopsided, untenable environments that will hold your relationship back.

It's time to replace these messages with a new one:

Our time has equal value.

My meetings and his meetings. The girls' socks and his Tweets. I'll explain.

Douglas and I had been playing a team game for a long time. His work schedule was flexible long before mine, and that allowed him to handle more sick days and doctor's appointments for our oldest daughter. When she was an infant, he even worked from home two days a week to save us money. But right as my career began to plateau, his firm started taking off and the weights on our scale began to shift. Under normal circumstances, we probably could have sorted it out. But what's normal to millennials, anyway? We live from one unprecedented time to the next.

In March 2020, our daughters were one and four, and Douglas was earning *at least three times* my salary. When the world shut down, I was working through many of the struggles we explored in the last two chapters, and I turned society's problems around on myself. He was earning so much more money than me, I felt obligated to do most of the unpaid labor. I became the Director of The Boneparth Cruise Ship to Nowhere, responsible for it all: food, entertainment, housekeeping, health, education, and risk management. I gave up at work. The expert you'll meet in a minute said, I was "complicit in my own oppression."

My time became less valuable than his. We both built that landscape: me enabling him and him enjoying my care. On top of his actual work, Douglas also took up the platform formally known as Twitter, which added a new dimension to what he would eventually consider "work." I know his silly dad jokes were just a way to cope with everything going on, but they also became an excuse to check out of what was *actually* going on in his *actual* house. I took jokes on the chin about The Magic Laundry Bin that just miraculously emptied itself; the one he would step over while giggling at a meme on his phone. Him and Hazel called me The Horse—a workhorse—huffing around the house while they played under my nose.

You can assume this all became less funny over time. The mental and physical load compounds. One bad day becomes a sock mountain of bad days with new pairs thrown on top.

I tried staying *hashtag grateful* but I also wanted to kill him. I was stretched too thin, no longer the lawyer I recognized or the mother I wanted to be. The conversation that needed to happen felt much bigger than who'd put in the Instacart order, and I didn't know how to start it. Not with people dying and the sky still falling.

So, I just got angrier and let it all build up, until one drunken night in Japan when he ordered a croissant... oh wait, that wasn't us. We were stuck at home. My croissant was a sock ball abandoned on the steps for three days.

But really, Douglas and I were rock solid for years. How could our marriage implode over a sock?

Eve Rodsky asked herself the same thing. For her, it wasn't socks—it was blueberries. A nonchalant text from her husband left her sobbing in her car, wondering not why she forgot her husband's smoothie produce but why—in a family with two powerhouse professionals—she was the one managing the entire

16. DIVIDE AND CONQUER

household load. She created *Fair Play*, which is now a book, a game, a documentary, and if you ask me, a movement, to level-set time and create a fairer division of labor in every home.

Her work changed the way we think about everything. So, you can imagine how excited I was to speak with her.

"For women to step into their full power in the world, whether it's financially or not, we have to invite men to step into their full power in the home," she said.

How you handle time together is no different than how you handle money together.

When you view time as a level playing field, you can start to see how the money you earn is just one component of how you contribute. Earning money is labor. So is holding your child's hand in the drop-off line at school.

Your contributions can be physical, mental, and financial. Seeing through this more holistic lens sheds light on all the ways we care for each other. You can only determine what is fair when you're considering all the visible and invisible tasks that consume your time.

Once you get your minds right, you still need to have a plan. This is no different than budgeting and cash flow. Couples who just "wing" how they divvy up responsibilities end up reacting, which leads to more conflict and does nothing to relieve your mental load.

I won't reinvent the wheel when Rodsky's card system is an excellent gamified way to visualize and reassign more than 100 household tasks that you've probably never considered in this level of detail. If you are looking for help in a way that feels fun, buy them. There's no better tool.

Our greatest takeaway from her groundbreaking system is ownership. Douglas always did "whatever I asked him to do," but swooping in at the eleventh hour to finish the job wasn't going to relieve the emotional labor I had already put in. In Rodsky's system, when you hold a card, you must *conceptualize*, *plan*, and *execute* the whole task. It's yours from start to finish.

This is how Douglas became Swim Dad. For Hazel's competitive swim team, Douglas pays registration, orders the team bathing suits, coordinates carpool to practice, and reads the emails all season. I get to walk into the meets, and my only job is to cheer for our daughter.

Ownership is crucial to a fairer division of labor, but when it comes to money, it's important to distinguish between owning a task and staying engaged. One of you can pay the bills, but both of you need to know how to access your money. One of you can renew your family's health insurance plan, but you both need to know what it covers.

You can delegate tasks from top to bottom, but you can't delegate your knowledge of money. There's an expense component to almost every task you perform; so, in order to accomplish these tasks with the context of your own financial lives, you still have to know what you're working with.

Honestly, I believe the reason many women turn a blind eye to their finances is because they're drowning in responsibilities that their partners should be sharing with them. Money might feel like the only thing they *don't have to worry about*. I get it. When I was drowning in tasks, I let my involvement slip, too. But reworking our contributions freed up my mental and actual space to become engaged in our finances again.

Like so much in this book, the hardest part is communicating about things that need to change.

"This is a highly triggering topic, especially when you're talking about caregiving and unpaid labor," Rodsky said. She told me a story about a pandemic-era Facebook group called something like, "Reasons I Hate My Partner and Kids During Covid," in which thousands of members showed up to complain about their spouses. When Rodsky DM'ed one of them to request to speak with her

16. DIVIDE AND CONQUER

and her husband about domestic life, she replied, there's nothing to talk about—they didn't talk about domestic life. This internet group was her safe space. "I think it's really important to recognize that publicly threatening to murder her husband in front of 27,000 strangers felt safer to her than communicating directly with her partner," Rodsky remarked.

That poster isn't alone. I've scrolled through hours of content in which creators lament or make jokes about their lack of support at home. These posts aren't funny. They're just desensitizing people into putting Band-Aids on big problems.

My friend Lindsey Stanberry, author of *Money Diaries*, set out to show how real couples divide responsibilities at home in her newsletter, *The Purse*. She calls this day-in-the-life series, "Division of Labor." I asked whether she thought these detailed accounts can move the needle to promote more equitable households. Some people, she believes, gain a lot from being able to see how other couples break it down. Some people probably realize they're putting up with too much. We all love to compare, even though none of our circumstances are quite the same.

By not addressing the unfair division of labor in your relationship, you're allowing it to continue. Rodsky brought up a great point: whether you know it or not, you're already communicating. You're snapping at the kids. You're huffing up the stairs with your big basket of laundry. Your resentment *shows*, and you owe your partner the chance to understand why you're so pissed off.

Couples therapist Brianna Brunner explained to me how we have primary and secondary emotions. Your primary emotions are what you experience first: in this case, you might be exhausted and upset from doing the lion's share of the household tasks day in and out. But when you don't communicate them, your secondary emotions—maybe anger, rage—do the talking. Those feelings aren't constructive, because they're not what you're really dealing with.

Timing is everything. Rodsky and Brunner both suggest you leave those heated moments where they are. Don't react. Divide and conquer tasks when emotion is low and cognition is high. Schedule a weekly or bi-weekly meeting time to connect when you're both able to pay attention without the noise of your lives ringing in your ears. Your regular household meetings will also prevent you from making reactive choices, which just like with your finances, can be counterproductive.

Our scale began to tip in Douglas's favor long before an avalanche of socks knocked the whole thing over. That doesn't mean it was always unfair. At one point, our decisions were conscious. We were fine with them. Years later, I wasn't. Too much had changed.

Fair is too fluid to ever be even. You don't achieve fairness in your home just once. You have to rebalance the scale all the time, because your lives and needs are constantly evolving. You may have to experiment and readjust until you find the right thing, and only you two will know what that is.

"Division of labor comes down to personal values," Stanberry said. "There's no one right way to do it, and I think striving for 50/50 is probably impossible."

Fair is a breakdown of responsibilities that you both believe you can handle; you both feel good about; and that allows you to preserve your individual senses of self.

It's one thing to lose yourself to parenthood. It's another to lose yourself to laundry.

Your time has value, and if you don't have enough of it, shuffle the deck.

17.
A NEW RECIPE

*Stepparents wear many hats.
They can fill many voids, too.*

The original title of this book was *The Merge*. As in, two people in a serious relationship are merging their financial lives, their beliefs, and their families. It had a little buzz to it. Felt cute. Might delete later. Which we did.

In learning some of people's most intimate reasons why they are the way they are, I realized that *merging* cannot be the ultimate goal of a relationship. That would suggest that two people should disappear into one another instead of maintaining the conviction of their independent selves. Choosing to marry your values together—and how you do that—is a conscious choice. Whatever new thing you create together doesn't erase the things you've created before.

Also, how would you merge into a second marriage? Would it mean you've unmerged only to re-merge again? Are you supposed to just fold your second spouse into the sourdough of your life and hope the baggage bakes off?

By the time I spoke with Lorna Hecht-Zablow, a licensed

marriage and family therapist, I already knew we'd have a new title, but her reaction to my use of the term "blended families" drove it home. "When you bring together families with disparate histories, and you think you're supposed to put them in a blender and churn them right out as this homogenous unit, that's where the conflict is going to come in," she said.

So, no merging *and* no blending. Got it.

I am comfortable leaving these terms behind, because in a sense, it alleviates some pressure from what everyone thinks they need to do, or who everyone thinks they need to be. This is particularly true with second marriages and those involving children from prior relationships.

Finding love, perhaps for a second time, people become very concerned with how they'll contribute to the lives of their partner's children. It's an awkward dance for everyone involved. You might feel like you're trying to fit a square peg in a round hole, and the stakes are incredibly high to get them to *just fit, dammit*. But with a broader view of what it means to contribute—to new members of your family, too—you can offer them abundance in more ways than one.

We should start with the actual money, though.

As with some other topics in this book, we can't offer partners who have been previously married or have children from prior relationships one right way to handle money in your new relationship. Your personal circumstances are just too factually dependent on your prior marriages, your children's needs, your financial health, and of course, whatever your legal documents say you should do. Let's stay on legal documents for a moment, because this is important.

Written agreements can speak for you—especially when you're worried about what to say. This is another circumstance where I hope to remove some of the negative stigma around contracts and let them do what they're supposed to do.

17. A NEW RECIPE

Settlements from prior marriages as well as pre-nuptial agreements both go a long way in outlining the expectations and obligations around how adults financially support their biological children and stepchildren. Like in *Beginnings*, when we discussed couples from disparate wealth backgrounds, expectations are everything. The more you outline in writing, the less there is to talk about later.

How specific you should get in these agreements depends on the whole cast of relevant characters, including: you, your ex, your family lawyer, your new partner, your therapist, your dry cleaner, whoever is relevant. Again, it's too personal for me to decide for you. Just consider that including more details means you've made more difficult decisions upfront. Less detail means you trust that the parties can make fair decisions as issues arise in the years to come.

I would approach these choices with a long runway; meaning, don't be naïve to the fact that feelings change over time. You and your ex might play nice in the sandbox *before* you've found a new partner. You and your second husband might not think you need to talk about college when your kids from prior marriages are four and six. Maybe you don't, but think long.

Once you have accomplished this, be done—*done*, done. Do whatever you need to do to move past your emotional challenges before your feelings bleed into the lives of your kids. And if you're a stepparent who is not a party to an agreement that may still impact your financial life, sorry. Address it in your own agreement, or let it go. You will most certainly impact the lives of your stepkids by trying to rewrite history on something that's settled.

But enough with that. Onto the good.

You can contribute more than money to your stepchild's life.

The main reason to not focus on an ambiguous goal of blending your families is to hold space for individual relationships to form. Hecht-Zablow believes the most important thing for stepparents to do is develop one-on-one relationships with every member of their new family. Don't clump together stepsiblings as "The Kids," she says. They aren't a flock of geese.

Putting in the effort to know them individually will reveal what they need from you and what role you can fill in their lives. In my case, I became a stepchild as a teen. There's a significant age gap between my dad and Melissa—she was never going to be a mother figure to me. But over the years, we've developed empathy for one another. We've created memories together and laughed a lot. She loves our daughters to no end. It took her a while to realize this, but she could play an important role in my family. Now, she does.

The best example I can offer you, though, is Laura and Susan. Their love story belongs in a song—or maybe, a drum circle. They met more than 30 years ago "in the middle of impossibilities," under the stars at a women's retreat.

See, Laura was married to a man, with two kids at home. After a traumatic childhood once had her homeless and suicidal, Laura met a kind, caring Myles and did what young people did in the Nineties down south: she got married and had kids. Conforming was hard for her, but that was the path to raising her kids in a safer environment than she had grown up in. Years later, she came out to her therapist, and then to Myles.

"We didn't have a bad marriage," she said. "We liked each other—we loved each other." Their plan was to stay together until the kids went to college; that was, until Laura met Susan that night under the stars. "I saw my future. It was terrible, because she was here way too early."

Laura returned home from the retreat, turned to her husband and said, *you're never going to believe this.*

He said, *I better meet her then.*

Susan came over for dinner. He loved her, and that was that.

Within months, Laura, Susan, two kids, two dogs, and two cats, were living in Susan's 900-square-foot house. "Back then for lesbians, it was hard to have kids," Susan explained. "When I met

17. A NEW RECIPE

them, my maternal instinct turned right on. I just felt maternal, and my parents were thrilled."

No one wished for Susan to replace Myles, and she didn't, but she did offer a lot of herself to her new family. Myles paid child support when he could, but Susan carried the financial load through her massage business while Laura got started in financial services. "If you think of it like a pie, we all sort of filled in," Laura said, alluding to much more than money. One person took summer camp. Another took back to school clothing. "Her mom filled in as a grandmother like you wouldn't believe. The family just filled in the pieces."

Like a pie. Got it.

View this as an opportunity, not an obligation. We lead rich lives because of the people in them, and if you never try, you'll never know.

That doesn't mean it's always easy. A risk of conflict always exists in any parent or parent-figure relationship. But as a stepparent, you should be allowed to impart your wisdom and values around money onto your stepkids.

Hecht-Zablow acknowledges that this might actually be hardest for the biological parent. Letting other people guide or discipline your children is tough, particularly when you'd prefer to keep the temperature low. But think about it: teachers, friends, lots of people hold influence over your children, whether you like it or not. Stepparents can provide a fresh and new perspective, and they don't need to undermine anyone else's lessons to do that.

Hecht-Zablow offered one more, hard dose of truth on this point that really stuck with me. If you aren't comfortable enough with your partner's judgment to let them work through an issue with your child, why are you even together?

I can't say I disagree.

Second spouses are also valuable in how they address blind spots in your own parenting. Take Walter, who was left to raise his two children as a virtual single father. He was in survival mode for a long time. When Petra came into their lives, she was able to see things the kids needed that he couldn't see. She pushed Walter to have their son, who is neurodivergent, enroll in a program that would assist him with social skills and helped him explore his love of the drums by finding him lessons. She exposed both the kids to theater and found other cultural opportunities to enrich their lives. Walter said it best:

> As a dad, I felt like I was always getting side eye, especially from moms, like that I was sort of not legitimate. And while I resented that, I also kind of understand that there were times where I just wasn't equipped. I didn't know which direction to go, and I was really sort of stuck in a valley of indecision. There were some key times when Petra—even though they're not her biological kids—stepped in like the mom they didn't have and said, this is what needs to happen to help these kids out.

Her input benefitted them all.

Aim for a seat on your stepchild's board of directors. My dad introduced me to this concept, and it's stuck with me my whole life.

Think about the people you turn to for advice. Not everyone's opinions should matter equally to you, but these are the people whose input you take to heart. They are the people whose perspective and support you lean on most.

I hope your partner is there. Beyond that, I encourage you to think critically about who belongs there. Your mother, your sister, your best friend might all be on your board, but they might not be. Title alone doesn't earn you a spot. A stepparent is the perfect example of someone who does not have a presumed seat but can earn one.

With the right recipe, you can contribute meaningfully to your stepchild's life. It might take some trial and error, but when you get there, you'll all know how sweet it is.

18.
FULL CIRCLE

You might not care for them today, but you will someday. Make sure you know who will help.

So far, in *Contributions*, we've focused on your kids. But providing for a nuclear family only represents one way to care. When other people you love need help, you ask what you can do. Your care becomes a web; it starts in the center with you and goes where you must take it. You don't only get to care downward. You care up. You care out. Love may bring you to care for someone you don't even know yet.

In the United States, people are living longer, but not without help. In 2021, a staggering 38 million caregivers were providing unpaid care valued at $600 billion, according to an AARP report.[46] Much of this care takes place for adults older than 65 who need help with routine tasks, medical advocacy, emotional support, and companionship, which seems to hit right around the time when all the stuff in the last four chapters happens. About a quarter of U.S. adults fall within this "sandwich generation," who have a parent older than 65 and children under 18 (or older than 18 but still receiving financial support).[47] This doesn't account for the many more who assume long-term responsibility for an adult sibling or relative with special needs. As anyone who has ever stepped into these roles can attest, it's a lot.

Not only has navigating healthcare systems gotten more complicated over time but so have the financial lives of today's unpaid caregivers. I could point to higher education, housing, childcare, and even groceries to illustrate how rising costs can saddle a couple's ability to accommodate just one additional dependent. This is a notable difference from past generations.

For example, categorically higher student loan ledgers and the current housing market have stood in the way of many millennials purchasing homes. Because we live and relocate to places for work that provide the greatest return on our education, we're often farther away from the place we once called home. The same village we sorely miss in our early days of parenting will call upon us, and the decisions we have to make become more complex than ever.

Some people are raised to believe it's their responsibility to care for their extended family: the question is not whether, but how. This isn't everyone.

Just as many people are truly conflicted over the level of financial support, emotional involvement, and care they can provide. When it becomes a source of conflict between siblings and spouses, it can change the whole dynamic of your family.

You and your partner probably have mental lists of the people you might need to care for someday. Maybe you've never discussed them, or you've tiptoed around them then left it alone. I understand the desire to put this off as long as you can. *Not a today problem*, you think. You're trying to preserve the *status quo* in your own life, afford the things you want, and worry about the people right in front of you first. This doesn't make you a bad person, but tomorrow becomes today, and you may not get to choose when.

Together, take stock of everyone who might need your care in

18. FULL CIRCLE

the future. For some couples, the list could be overwhelming, but at least you're being realistic about your potential responsibilities down the line. No matter how young you are or how far away you think the time will be, you can at least agree on broad expectations, because they're rooted in your values above anything else.

Walking through this door is undoubtedly sensitive. We are talking about people—not just expenses—and you both have your own feelings about them. These are parents who raised you. Siblings who have loved you. Friends who have stepped up when no one else did. Your partner should recognize the weight of those bonds; however, that can't be the end of your process.

From your partner's standpoint, if they don't have great relationships with some people on your list, that might impact how they feel about supporting them. Your partner's voice should be heard not only with you but in conversations with your siblings, and potentially, the people to be cared for. The earlier you start, the more time you have to mend bridges and prevent new cracks from forming in your own relationship and those with your extended family members.

I spoke with Alexandria Nadworny, a CFP® professional who specializes in helping families plan a lifetime of care for individuals that may not be able to provide for themselves now or in the future. The mission is personal to her: Nadworny's brother has Down Syndrome and is supported by her parents. Alex will proudly step into that role someday. She lives what she teaches her clients about preparing for then.

"We focus on the vision first," she said. What does "caring" for someone look like as that person's life progresses? Are they living independently but closer to you? Are they living *with* you? Will they need resident housing with progressive levels of support? And that's just housing. How many times a week will you want to see them? What sustains the quality of their life?

What sustains yours?

Camryn and Jeff didn't have a vision—or much time for a plan.

In 2015, Camryn's mother, Josephine, was living in Chicago when she was diagnosed with Parkinson's Disease. Josephine was a single mom for most of Camryn's life, raising three children while earning a Ph.D. and two master's degrees as a psychotherapist. She was a vegetarian who finished triathlons.

"When you see me post about Mom on social media, it was because she was amazing, and I don't know how she did it," Camryn said. It was hard for any of them to imagine her being anything other than who she was.

Camryn and her siblings decided that Camryn would be the one to care for their mom as her disease progressed. Jeff was informed of this when his relationship with Camryn got serious, but neither of them really knew what it meant. They thought Michael J. Fox was a vision of their future, when his experience is just one direction that Parkinson's can take. "I was in denial when I said I was going to take care of my mom," she said. "I had no idea this would be the road."

Three years into her diagnosis, Josephine suffered a fall. She needed to move sooner than they thought. Camryn and Jeff had just moved to North Carolina for her job, and she was pregnant with their first child. After just two years of marriage, Josephine moved into their 1,300 square-foot townhome.

"It just felt so scary when she was 70 years old to be like, 'I'm going to put you in a home,'" Camryn said. "I couldn't do it." As a result, they abruptly took on the disease's unknowns, including her mother's surprising cognitive decline. Camryn gave birth, and within months, they were parenting two humans for the first time.

Aim for an evolution—not an event. When you're planning for someone's care, you want to maintain continuity for everyone involved. "That's the goal: to have it evolve over time, to pass the baton," Nadwordy told me. "Whether for an aging individual or for someone with special needs, you don't want the care stopped

18. FULL CIRCLE

by one person and then picked up by another the next day." When you wait for the next event, you're acting under duress. Any decisions you make regarding your time and resources won't be as measured as they should be. They might be flat out wrong.

At the time, Camryn and Jeff thought they were evolving. They built a custom home with accessible space to accommodate Josephine, thinking she'd live out her years with them. Camryn resumed her busy travel schedule for work, making Jeff her primary caregiver. He's a natural who would do anything for the people in his life. But leaving Jeff in charge wasn't a transition—it was a reaction.

"That wasn't really a joint decision on our part," Jeff said. "Camryn has rightly described her mom as a saint, a wonderful woman who got dealt the shittiest hand you possibly could be dealt. So, I want her to have a standard. And in the absence of getting that from someone else, I stepped into it, to the detriment of myself at times."

Wanting someone you love to maintain as much independence as possible is an empathetic goal, but protecting other people matters, too, said our friend Michael Greenberg, a trusts and estates attorney who specializes in elder care. Greenberg's own father, an endodontist, was diagnosed with Alzheimer's Disease at 56. He was performing surgeries one day, and the next, he was forced to retire. Of course, it was devastating. But like removing a driver's license from someone who can no longer see, you as a caregiver need to consider everyone else.

Josephine started hallucinating. She was seeing people out the window. One day, she took the baby out of her crib and accused Jeff of kidnapping her. Camryn returned home from work trips to find Jeff exasperated and exhausted. He'd been sounding the alarm bell on Josephine for too long and gave his wife an ultimatum: they couldn't have another baby until Mom had a new place to live.

Camryn and Jeff were lucky in a sense: Josephine was oversold on a long-term care insurance policy years ago, which offset the financial burden of increasing her care. She was able to move into an assisted living facility with supplemental help from an outside caregiver, who Camryn said, "was the most important person in our lives."

But I don't have enough space to capture the toll this had taken on Jeff. During our interviews, you could see it all over him. He won't call it regret—he's too loving for that—but he mourns his own personal losses. There are years of early fatherhood he can't recreate.

Camryn described it in stark terms. Unlike the joy of raising their daughter, "My mom did not grow up and become independent. It was the exact opposite."

The invisible costs of care hit hard. Without trying to have Josephine live with them, they wouldn't have paid for a custom home. Camryn wouldn't have needed to earn as much. Jeff wouldn't have burned out so hard between jobs. For seven months while looking for new remote work, "I was dead," he said. "I felt like I had drained my battery so low that I just wanted to sit in a room and not do anything or talk to anyone." Jeff needed support, too.

Support is a full circle. The right care team will envelop not only the person being cared for, but the primary caregivers, too.

Alexandria Nadworny's financial practice helps families identify "as many people who were part of a person's life, so that there can be a rolodex of people that can be reached out to depending on the circumstances." Formal roles include legal representatives, which we'll touch on in the next chapter. Informal roles might include a care manager, social worker, benefits specialist, maybe even former colleagues or friends, or other caregivers who are in similar situations as you.

Camryn and Jeff, for example, started paying their financial advisor to submit all of the reimbursement claims for Josephine's

18. FULL CIRCLE

care. But they still had a blind spot: Josephine's circle of support needed to include giving Jeff enough space to reclaim his own life.

In searching for a nanny, he said, "I need to be more honest that I can't have it all without someone helping me. Whether it's important for the value I get from it, or to get me in a good enough place to provide that value to the people around me."

They know it hurt their marriage.

"I look at Camryn with nothing but love for her," he said. "But this has complicated our lives so much that I can't look at Camryn and say just, *this is my wife, and I love her*. I say, *I love you, and I wish you were home more*."

He was saying, I need your help. I lost myself in all of this.

What Camryn and Jeff have gone through underscores the importance of starting years earlier than you think you'll need to. Take stock now—there's no reason to wait—and then have meaningful conversations with the people who you'll be caring for. If they have adequate financial and physical health, they might qualify for long-term care insurance, which can alleviate some of your financial burdens down the road. If that's not an option, you can still begin assembling their circle of support long before you need to make concrete decisions about their care. You can plan with a long runway that even has several options, which account for where you're at in your own lives. In blunt force, this can be too much for your relationship to withstand. Gradual change is better.

Following our interviews, the family went through another transition: they welcomed a son.

We smile at their photos: a big healthy baby, a proud big sister, two parents who love each other finding their way home. Camryn's mom would sit beside them, her gentle hand on Baby DJ's head. A family come full circle.

19.
PAMELA

In your relationship's darkest hours, you see what you're truly capable of.

It's a strange but real phenomenon: the notion that the deeper you fall in love, the deeper you can fall into fear. How it transforms from affection to compulsion. When your most mundane Monday nights intertwine with theirs, you begin to question whether you desire their presence on your left side in bed or you require it. Whether you want them or need them. Half of me is now them. *Could I survive without them?*

I've asked myself this before. You might have, too.

My childhood conditioned me to look for moments before moments—fate's foreboding warnings when it's all about to change. Life can change in an instant, or a year, or five years. In any case, you'll be grasping at our most elusive currency: time.

Consider the following stories about living, not dying. When you're faced with a finite amount of time together, you have choices in how you use it. You can live with presence and face death with

19. PAMELA

intention. As a partner, you can do things you never thought you'd be capable of.

BEFORE

Symptoms. Waiting. Half answers. Waiting. Testing. It's an irregular cadence they can't find peace in. They need more information, but that doesn't mean they want the information they need.

Two wives received news about their husbands.

Ava's husband, Dean, had "potential ALS," the doctor's notes said, as if you could ever walk those three letters back.

Savannah's husband, Robert, had lesions all over his brain.

Just a few years ago, both couples were in the primetime of their lives. Ava and Dean purchased a 1950s ranch home in Nashville near his family. He was finally a firefighter. Their toddler was on the move. Meanwhile, Savannah and Robert had just had their "what if we have one more" child, a third. The digital marketing company they built from the ground up had just been acquired. They were building their dream home in their big university town.

The news shook up everything: who mattered; what mattered; when it mattered. Our hearts know how to renegotiate what we pray for.

Doctors thought Robert's pathology report would show anaplastic astrocytoma, with a prognosis of three-to-five years. Two weeks later, they called to say it was glioblastoma, the worst form of brain cancer, and gave no timeline at all.

"That kicked off 17 months of the craziest, I don't even want to say hell, because there was so much wonder and hope and joyful moments in it, too, which sounds so strange. But when you're going through life or death, I think all the noise gets pushed aside," Savannah said.

Both women leapt into action, suiting up at base camp of an

administrative Mount Everest. Savannah went to every doctor's appointment that she could and kept a running spreadsheet of Robert's medications. She had a good enough understanding of the healthcare system to run point, but even so felt "not prepared to navigate a disease like glioblastoma, where there isn't anything they can really give you." They flew to Germany several times for new personalized vaccine therapies. Some of Robert's meds could get "off-label" approval to be covered by insurance as compassionate use drugs, but others, they had to pay for out of pocket. The same happened with outside help. Most therapies, Savannah said, only get insurance approval for patients who can *improve.* And most hired caregivers are meant for the elderly and are not available for families with three young kids at home. As his disease progressed, Savannah found an organization to provide therapists that could help physically care for Robert. They cost $200 per hour.

"I would just say over and over again how fortunate we were in the timeline that we sold our business," she said. "We had the financial resources to do this, and it makes me so sad to think about all the people who don't."

Ava and Dean don't have those same resources, but they do have Pamela.

See, from the minute the first doctor placed "potential ALS" in Dean's patient chart—taking him off the job but also precluding him from short-term disability benefits without a formal diagnosis—Pamela was making phone calls, sending letters, filing appeals. Her charm got Dean into the Mayo Clinic and Duke University for testing. Ava kept her day job while Pamela fought for Medicare approval. Her girlfriends joke that Pamela's not the nice girl you invite to a dinner party. She's scrappy and takes no shit.

Pamela is Ava's alter ego.

I kept thinking, *you don't need an alter ego, Ava. You're amazing as you are.* I told her this much, but she is too humble. She said

19. PAMELA

that I'm amazing for writing this book. I shudder at the thought of equating her experience with anything I've done. I am a mere receptacle of bravery like hers.

In these situations, I realize, whatever you must do to reconcile your fear, you'll do. But also, neither woman approached their husbands' challenges alone.

Dean is a doer. He's changed his diet, cut out alcohol, researches clinical trials. He shows Ava how to take down the Christmas lights and blow leaves from the gutter.

"He keeps looking at me and saying, 'You got this.' And I'm like, okay, I got this." She was going inward, at first, emotionally speaking. Now past the initial shock, she knows they need to be open with each other to brace for what's to come.

"I don't cry alone anymore," she said.

I think about that a lot.

Savannah and Robert were no different. "From day one, we decided that even though he was the one sick, it was going to be a journey we were on together," Savannah said. For a while, his scans looked stable, but Robert felt his mind beginning to deteriorate. He started asking for help, but it was more than help. He knew he was passing the baton on tasks he would never resume.

They talked a lot about his wishes. About what it means to *live* versus *exist*.

Robert told her, "It's not so much I fear death itself but a long, drawn-out demise." They formalized their estate plans, quickly, without hesitation. Savannah carried his words around on a piece of paper when Robert could no longer communicate. They were the most important instructions she'd ever been given, and she wasn't going to let anyone undermine them. She'd been the one living his decline, day after day. He wanted her to be able to let go, and he trusted her to know when.

Comparing two diseases, two prognoses, two couples, two caregivers... it's impossible. Medical time horizons can cloud your senses, and on a more basic level, people process their feelings in different ways.

Jill Cohen, a family grief counselor in New York City, talked to me about anticipatory grief, which is how people mourn before a loss. These are powerful emotions that can impact not just how you feel, but how you fight, and how you plan.

At the time I spoke with Ava, this was all so new. Dean's grief from receiving his diagnosis was fresh. He was supposed to join us for our interview, though I understood when only Ava appeared on Zoom that night. I could feel his presence just beyond the screen.

Dean didn't want to think about next steps. He didn't want to modify the house. He didn't want to take steps to preserve his voice. He didn't want to prepare a will. It all felt like giving up.

"You don't want to make someone already uncomfortable more uncomfortable," Ava said. "But I got pissed and was like, I'm asking and begging you to do these things, and you need to do them. That's when Pamela was like, *cry as much as you want, you're doing it.*"

Michael Greenberg, the estate planning attorney, sees this often. **The documents to any basic estate plan include a: (1) will; (2) health care proxy; (3) power of attorney; and if you have kids, (4) a minor's trust built into the will**. These legal vehicles are crucial to making sure your wishes are followed and your assets end up where they're supposed to end up. We cannot overstate how wrong things can go for couples who don't see this through. Find a Michael Greenberg now. Don't wait for moments like these.

If your partner resists estate planning for any reason, Greenberg says, make it about you. Particularly if your partner is sick and resists because he feels like you're planning for his death. You are not. You are protecting your life, your livelihood, your family. Have him do it for you.

Life-threatening moments are life-affirming, too. I want you to see that.

Both women spoke with me about how quickly their

19. PAMELA

priorities changed. Things that seemed so important before just weren't anymore.

Savannah and Robert wanted their new home so badly, but he was sick by the time they got the keys. At closing, she remembers him falling quiet, and she asked him what was wrong.

He said, this is the house they'll bring me out of.

I think about that a lot, too.

With a terminal illness, a house is just a house. It's not what matters anymore. Having your best friends over for a barbeque matters. Playing games with your children matters. Memories matter. Material possessions don't.

You can begin learning the language of grief before death. Cohen says that you can maximize the quality of the time you have together by continuing on with the things you love to do the most. She told me about a couple in New York City who were regulars at a hotel restaurant down the block from their apartment. When the husband fell ill, she encouraged them to keep going, even if they had to take a cab just two short blocks. Make accommodations, but keep doing it.

"At the end of the day, we are all born, and we are all going to die, but we don't know when. Robert also knew he was going to die, and he didn't know exactly when. We're all pretending we know it's a little longer," Savannah said, overwhelming me with truth. "I was not focused on death and focused on him being here today. What can we do to feel alive today?"

Ava and Dean are still learning their language of grief, but she won't wish away even their saddest days, which are yet to come.

I had one last question for Ava; the one I asked almost everyone. I really didn't want to, but I think she would've been pissed to find out I was too afraid to ask a hard thing when they're doing such hard things. I guess I found a little Pamela in me, too.

I asked whether they have enough.

"No," she said. "We don't have enough time."

AFTER

I spoke with Savannah after a family trip to Europe. It was restorative for all of them, but especially her. She felt like, for the first time in a while, people weren't looking at her with pity. She was just another person exploring the world with her kids.

Robert's death was something she knew would come, but she couldn't comprehend until it came. He was her anchor. Without him, she was adrift.

"My whole life revolved around making him comfortable, keeping him alive, then finding a cure, keeping him alive, and making him comfortable again, in that order," she said. "It was so centered around him, and then he's gone. It's like the world revolves around the sun, and then the sun disappears. You know, like, what am I revolving around now?"

Grief has been a journey filled with surprises. Often, the little things hurt the most.

Savannah and Robert had a buttoned-up estate plan, but estate plans don't cover the details of everyday life: the landscaper's phone number; the schedule for cleaning your appliances. These are invisible ways we care for each other until a gaping omission makes them known.

Savannah had finally been able to close Robert's credit card, forgetting it was still linked to their Netflix account. When she sat down for a movie night with their kids and they couldn't log in, it devastated them all over again. Little things become big things when grief wants them to.

In relationships, death is not just heartbreak but disruption. Even when you have all your affairs in order legally speaking, there's still so much unspoken for. Grief arises in missing passwords, subscriptions you can't cancel, social media accounts you can't take down. I cannot comprehend the fortitude it takes to care about

19. PAMELA

these tiny things when your heart is shattered; and yet, ignoring them is not a permanent option. Your circle of support can only help if they've got the blueprint of what to help you with.

My personal anxieties around death prompted Douglas to prepare his most loving letter to me ever—more thoughtful and considerate than any card or post. It is a document that outlines, in painstaking detail, how I can continue our lives in the event he is gone. "Sorry I am dead," he starts it, true to form. He'll always keep me laughing, but with this information, he'll keep us going, too.

A death note is a love letter. Consider it a business continuity plan for your life.

In ours, Douglas lists the names and contact information of every crucial person I should contact in the immediate aftermath of his death: attorneys, advisors, our accountant, business contacts, and close friends with specific responsibilities they can assist with. He includes the login credentials to his devices and password manager. And yes, he even outlines his wishes for his beloved social media accounts.

Don't worry about oversharing in this document—assume your partner knows nothing, to be sure they know everything. I've even told Douglas which friend of ours I'd like to help him shop for the girls' clothing. It seems granular now, but it wouldn't feel that way if he needed it.

People say things to grief counselors like, "half of me died when my husband died." But Cohen assures them, "half of you is still alive."

She focuses on continuing bonds between people, even after death. "How you live was informed by your relationship. You did this together." The way you raise your kids, the way you show up for people, even the way you approach money, all derive from a value system you built together. Outlining everything for your partner allows your bond to endure through continuing your daily practices, as you've always done. You are smoothing the edges to help them find peace.

I asked Savannah the same question: about enough. Her answer amazed me.

She said, their lives have been incredibly sad, but they get to choose whether they're bad. In that context, "I think the whole idea of happiness and contentment comes from focusing not on what you *don't* have and focusing on what you *do* have. So, my answer would be 100% yes, I feel like I have everything I need to make a happy life. Yes."

In terms of grief, Savannah's therapist tells her she's not in a pit—she's in a tunnel. The light will appear again someday. She just has to keep walking.

YOUR QUESTIONS ON CONTRIBUTIONS

1. What season of life are you in right now?
2. Do you need to reprioritize your goals to meet this moment?
3. Are you using your time the way you'd like to be?
4. How do you contribute to your household?
5. What percentage of the household tasks do you own?
6. What percentage of the mental labor do you bear?
7. Could you execute on your partner's responsibilities at home?
8. List everyone you might need to care for someday.
9. Do you have a: (1) will; (2) power of attorney; (3) health care proxy; and (4) living will?
10. What would your partner need to know if you weren't here?

PART IV.
POWER

Over the next six chapters, we'll call power by its name.
Power plays a major role in our relationships. As partners, you have a chance to empower one another. As individuals, you have an obligation to access your own power. There are sources of power, such as money, and quests for power in your ambition. There are institutions that hold power over us. There are people who do, too.

Turning away from your own power is how you check out. How your needs stay unmet, and you remain unseen. For your relationship to be fair, your voice must be heard, so we will share with you the ways to step into your own power with money. Only when you both own these tools will you have the power to really work together.

Our careers can have a powerful hold over us, and you'll see that here. You can reap incredible rewards when you play a team game, but investing in one partner's work often demands the other's sacrifice in some form. The powers of ego, of gender, of expectations, are very real. We can get so caught up in one identity—in one image of ourselves—that it's hard to move on when the time comes.

We also let a lot of noise into our relationships that shouldn't be there. These days, information and consumption are one and the same. The messages we receive online wield power over us before we even realize how damaging they can be.

Let's see.

20.
OUR TINY REBELLIONS

Before you can become an unstoppable financial team, you both need to step into your power with money. Here's how you do it.

On the wall of a spa, I once read: "Balance is not something you find. It is something you create."

Four years ago, I would've written that in my newsletter with zero irony whatsoever. Each week, I wrote about flowers and jogging and baking with our girls, while managing my workload and laundry load and an invisible, emotional load. I wrote thousands of words about the little blessings in our lives, of which there were plenty, but inside I felt like I was taking hit after hit.

Perhaps I was just shrinking myself to be palatable enough to survive in all the spaces that only want women the way they want us. Places that tolerate us but don't support us. I was growing sick of needing permission to shine at work, at home, or anywhere else.

I wrote everything but what had to be said: I didn't want to feel small anymore.

As we begin exploring *Power* in all its forms, let me offer you this to think about first:

Before you can address the power dynamics in your relationship, you need to step into your own power as an individual.

It's not something you find. It's something you create.

Most people reduce the concept of power in relationships to which person has power over the other. Certainly, we will talk about that. But creating fairness between two people isn't limited to taking from one to give to the other. Harnessing your individual power offers a deep assurance in your sense of self. This power helps you identify your wants and needs and gives you the confidence to assert them in your relationship.

Dr. Mona DeKoven Fishbane, a licensed clinical psychologist, wrote about how power can *empower* partners to connect with more mutual support for each other. She acknowledges that our cultural assumptions about power pit us against our spouses in perpetual struggle: *it's either him or me who can get what they want.*

"Traditional notions of power—related to physical size, gender, earning capacity, class, education, etc.—are about Power Over, the power of one person to dominate or influence another," she wrote. "Power Over" thinking is what we know. It's a win or lose game.

Instead, Dr. Fishbane proposes we draw upon our personal ability to make choices that align with our values. We all have a certain "Power To," as she states, act with "flexibility, thoughtfulness, self-regulation, responsiveness, and responsibility." Working on our individual "Power To" strengthens our emotional intelligence and puts us in a position to "speak [our] own feelings, beliefs, and needs, in a manner that also holds concern for the other and the relationship."

We can then bring our personal work together to hone our

20. OUR TINY REBELLIONS

"Power With," which is our mutual obligation to cultivate and care for the relationship. She writes, both partners need to have empathy, learn how to apologize, and understand that even healthy relationships go through cycles of rupture and repair.[48]

Self-awareness is a critical first step.

I spoke with Dr. Alexandra Solomon, a licensed clinical psychologist, about the concept of relational self-awareness. She calls it, "an ongoing exploration of our relationship to relationships." Looking in the mirror can strengthen bonds with our kids, colleagues, and friends; but most of all, it creates the foundation for a solid intimate partnership. Everyone knows it's much easier to focus on your partner's baggage than your own, "but we can't begin to heal and feel empowered until we start to understand our own inner landscape."

We should be calling power out by name. Try to understand where your individual powers lie—or lack—to better contextualize the feelings playing out in your relationship. Only then can you see clearly whether any fixes should come from you, your partner, or a collaboration between you both.

This is a complex topic, if you couldn't tell already. But I like how Dr. Solomon has couples think about power that is "ascribed" and power that is "achieved."

Ascribed power, she says, is baked into relationships. Think back to *Beginnings*, where we explored how everything from our attachment styles, to our cultures, to our financial privileges, to our traumas, can all inform our money beliefs as adults. We enter relationships with these differences baked in. They can be quiet, omnipresent, and hard to acknowledge.

But then, there's achieved power, which emerges during the course of your relationship. People often think about this kind of power as whoever's the "loudest in the room," but to confuse matters more, that's not always true. There's lots of ways partners take and cede control. The loudest person can actually feel quite powerless.

In the thick of our latest reckoning with power, I viewed my handsome, privileged, White Man in Finance husband who earned more money than me as having the good life, whereas I was proverbially shoveling shit. Though I felt powerless, I stomped around the house, yelling over his most trivial transgressions. He would then dissociate into his phone, flexing what I thought was his own power to keep things *status quo*. Had we retained one of the brilliant couples' therapists I've since come to know for this book, I would've realized that *he also* felt powerless, because he didn't know how to help me. And of course, we did a terrible job talking about it.

Our example says a lot about the power of assumptions. So did the stories of the couples we spoke with.

Throughout our interviews, a very gendered assumption about power kept rearing its head: women who earn less or no income felt less free to spend. They often defer to their male partners about making purchases, as if they are seeking permission. (I know. *Ick.*) Before you jump to blame their husbands, I'll share that many of them told me they encourage their wives to spend whatever they need on their families and themselves. Whether that's a whole or partial truth doesn't matter, because for one reason or another, the women are thinking it.

Mary Beth Storjohann, CFP®, understands the power of the voice in our own heads. To evolve past our limiting self-talk, we need to examine the difference between what we assume and what we believe. "A lot of people just carry forward societal assumptions, as opposed to doing the inner reflection and personal examination of asking, do I actually believe this?" she posed to me. "Do I believe that because I make less money, I should defer on my wants, and my partner who makes more money gets to pursue theirs?"

This isn't rhetorical.

20. OUR TINY REBELLIONS

Money is an essential vehicle of finding your power in your relationship. When you shy away from this, you are keeping so many of your needs, opinions, and options off the table. You have an obligation not only to yourself but to your partner to have your voice heard, because great partnerships require the work of two people.

The power to have a voice in your relationship begins with you:

your **knowledge;**
your **values;**
your **convictions.**

Don't look for those answers in your partner, your parents, your peers, or your assumptions. They belong to you.

We don't offer many *how to's* in this book, but these points are too important to leave open for interpretation.

Here are the ways to step into your power with money:

1. **Become intimate with your household finances—no matter who pays the bills.**
   Confidence comes from knowledge, period. No matter who handles the tasks related to money in your home, both of you share the responsibility to know what's there. I know this seems incredibly daunting if you've been disengaged for a while (or forever). So, let's break this goal down to some smaller steps you can achieve:

   - **Gain access to everything.** You should have the logins and passwords to all your financial accounts and systems. Save them securely to a password manager. If they have apps available for your phone, download them all. The easier your access, the more comfortable you'll become with checking in. Note: if your partner resists, ask questions. Frankly, it's a red flag, which you'll see at the end of this section.

- **Know these four things: (1) what you make; (2) what you spend; (3) what you have; and (4) what you owe.** These numbers are the most important pieces of information about your financial life and the context you need to have informed conversations about money with your partner.

- **Attend the meetings.** You are one-half of a couple who can retain the services of professionals like financial advisors, tax accountants, and estate planners. You should be there, always. No more assumptions should be made on your behalf.

- **Find ways to care that work for you.** Remember back in *Beginnings*, where we talked about meeting your partner where they are? Give yourself that same grace. You don't need a subscription to the *Financial Times* to learn a little more about money. There has never been more accessible content with a wider spectrum of voices on money than there is right now. Do you prefer newsletters? Audiobooks? Podcasts? YouTube channels? Just find what you like. Everyone needs to start somewhere.

2. **Set boundaries that honor the value of your time.**
You know this from *Contributions*: we are all contributors. We all provide. Our time has equal value no matter how much we earn. Still, it's hard to put this into practice each day.

"Whether they're the breadwinners or not, women tend to put themselves last," Storjohann mentioned, as we descended into The Most Relatable territory for us both. "Their stuff is typically the first to go off the calendar. They're the first to compromise on their goals—they will defer and push them

20. OUR TINY REBELLIONS

back." So many perceived obligations pile onto our dockets that it can feel like life is happening *to* us.

But everyone's allowed to strive for some non-negotiables at home and at work. If your partner's taking your kids out for the afternoon so you can do something that's important to you, remind them only to contact you in case of emergency. The same goes for work. When your tenth anniversary trip's been on the calendar for a year, turn your work phone on Do Not Disturb and prioritize that time. If the school principal's begging you to be the class parent because no one else has stepped up, that's unfortunate but "no, thank you!" is a complete sentence.

3. **Figure out what you want.**
Self-awareness is bigger than owning your flaws. People change. You're probably not the same person who met your partner years ago. Masking the ways you've evolved as an individual just to keep things comfortable diminishes your power.

Give yourself a chance to explore what you want as the person you are *right now*. What would be *enough* for you today—this very year?

Storjohann refers to this as dating yourself. "Especially if you've lost your power, you need to get to know yourself again," she said.

I love this question she asks her clients and include a version of it at the end of the section: "If we are meeting three years from today, what would have to happen (a) personally; (b) professionally; and (c) financially, for you to be happy with the progress you've made?"

Don't ever discount the right you have to be happy.

The confidence and sense of self you will gain in mastering these practices will help you build a stronger partnership.

Both Storjohann, as a financial advisor, and Dr. Solomon, as a couples therapist, offered similar perspectives on working with two people at the same time. In financial planning, Storjohann said she likes clients to "plan as individuals and then come together as a couple." Working this way accounts for the goals of each person, and then the joint goals they can strive for together. Many people skip the first step and end up appeasing their own wishes away.

Dr. Solomon made it even simpler: "I often talk about the golden equation of love: my stuff + your stuff = our stuff."

The whole thrives on the power of its parts.

Out of curiosity, I asked Dr. Solomon about the format of her book, *Love Every Day*, which offers 365 daily practices for couples to try for an entire calendar year. She chose it for two reasons. First, therapy heals people in microdoses. And second, love gains more strength in the small moments than the sweeping romantic gestures.

If you are staring at this chapter wondering how and where to begin, just know that we know, these changes aren't easy. Start small. Maybe you start in the order above, but maybe you don't. Maybe you start with answering the questions at the end of the section. Maybe you start with dinner. No matter how you start, it starts with you.

I think about my newsletter often, sitting idle like a time capsule from when I took on the massive endeavor of this book. Perhaps it's time for my reframe, too.

My tiny victories weren't fresh-baked cookies or wide-leg pants but the fact that I took three non-negotiable hours each week to reclaim my love of writing. I found a small-but-mighty audience who valued what I had to say. I built something that felt more important to me than almost anything I'd done in a decade, aside from having our beautiful daughters. My words were no cry for help. They were my steppingstones of power.

What will be yours?

21.
TWO SIDES, SAME COIN

Power couples share a collective ambition: my win is your win, and your win is mine.

When you think of the term "power couple," I'm sure you've got a notable duo that comes to mind. They might be celebrities, politicians, or businesspeople. You can take your own pick, because I'm not naming names. By the time you read this, there's too great a chance they either won't be together anymore, or we won't be allowed to celebrate them for one reason or another! Hollywood and Washington and Silicon Valley move too fast, as does our judgment of people.

Besides, we don't need to look that far. How I see it, you don't need global influence or *Fortune*-list wealth to embody the spirit of a "power couple." Out of all the couples we interviewed, those who helped me understand what the term means stood out because of their fluid roles in their relationships. At any given time, one partner will earn more than the other. Then, it flips. Wealth is a byproduct of their success, but money doesn't buy their entry into the club.

"Power couples" are two people who carry ambition, passion, and purpose as individuals, but truly embrace the power of the sum of their parts. They stand on their own two feet, but they feed off each other. They are better together.

Melissa Joy, CFP®, knows a power couple when she sees one. "They have the ability to be competent in any room they go into," she said. "They are used to being deciders—and when they don't intentionally decide, they delegate."

What an interesting synergy, once again, with the value of time. The couples I place under the "power couple" umbrella are all comfortable deploying funds to operate at a high level. For example, Clara (another financial advisor) and Ron (a medical director) outsource everything from doing the laundry, to grocery shopping, to preparing meals, to driving the kids around after school. Whatever it takes to keep the wheels moving.

Honestly, I think couples make these investments to sidestep conflict and avoid having to negotiate whose time matters more. We've been there ourselves. Douglas and I hired afternoon babysitters for years to avoid ending up in the same old conversation about who gets to keep working when school lets out. For the day-to-day, delegating does help. All is well when no one's feeling squeezed. But beyond goods and services, this fix has its limits. The time may come when you have to make a big sacrifice in order for your partner to invest in themselves.

Investment and sacrifice are two sides of the same coin.

This is a tough truth for career-driven couples. Many of us grew up in a culture of individualism that primed us to climb and compete from an early age.

When we spoke, Dr. Alexandra Solomon raised a great point: How many of us met our partners in school or at work? Some

21. TWO SIDES, SAME COIN

couples had to write the same papers and vied for the same promotions. Even if you're not in the same industry, this notion of maintaining forward momentum is so steeped in our existence, it's no wonder some people look to their spouses as the closest barometers of where they should be.

"It's so easy to slip into *me versus you*, especially because money and power are so culturally merged together," she said. We can deeply admire our spouses, but "we are primed to enter difficult conversations as a competition."

Instead, you should be striving for a collective ambition: my win is your win. Your win is mine.

Both couples I'm about to introduce value each other's careers without ego. They don't hold a mirror up to their partner's success and get consumed by how it makes them feel about themselves. Like a coin, their earning powers have flipped time and again. That doesn't disturb them. If anything, it helps them build off each other.

Jane, a psychologist, and Ashley, a start-up founder, are a true joint venture. Years ago, Jane left academia to support Ashley taking on a new job, but she kept building in the background. That's just what they do. She can tell you in her own words:

> We ladder each other up: one person is kind of the income generator, and the other is the builder, and then it swaps, and it swaps again. Our careers have leapfrogged like that with the support of the other person. I think we've both been 100% behind the other person's ambition and wanting them to be incredibly successful. Like, we're a team. If Ashley wins and I'm not doing well for some reason, we win. And if I'm doing well and she's struggling, we still win.

It didn't surprise me that they carry this ethos into their finances, too. Without hesitation, they write checks for each other's big things. They don't keep score. "We're not looking at our financial picture as mine or hers, it's really ours," she said. "All debt is ours. All future stuff is ours."

Even when you're so aligned, sacrifices still need to be made. Let's meet Kelsey and Scott.

Kelsey knew what she signed up for. They're both attorneys, but Scott is a legal scholar and tenured professor. Where he works, they go.

In Washington, D.C., they laid the early building blocks of their careers. Kelsey was on partner track at a fancy white-shoe law firm, but after nine years, they were both open to a lifestyle change. When Scott got hired at a large university in Texas, she was fully on board, even though she had to accept a 50% pay cut to work at a smaller regional firm. "We've never pursued paths solely for the purpose of what is going to make us the most money," she said. "But I think we had underestimated how much of a real hit to my career it might have been."

Texas is nothing like D.C., they learned. Kelsey would've most certainly been a Big Law partner had they stayed, but after their move, she really did have to start over. After a handful of years in private practice—even making partner at a mid-size firm—she transitioned into legal recruiting. She admits, she would've probably never had the luxury to consider a career change had they stayed put. Everything happens for a reason, but that doesn't mean it wasn't hard.

Having to relocate for work is a common source of conflict. To invest in one spouse's career opportunity in a new place, the other will be making an inherent sacrifice. It could look like getting passed over for a future promotion, having to leave a community of family and friends, downsizing your home in a higher cost-of-living area, I could go on. But the point is that these decisions don't get made in a vacuum. They can impact everything and need to be analyzed as if they will.

Dr. Marina Rosenthal, a licensed psychologist serving couples in

21. TWO SIDES, SAME COIN

high-conflict relationships, suggests you "buy time and don't rush" when making major life moves like this one. "A lot of resentment can breed when people make decisions under pressure."

Use your problem-solving skills to reach big decisions. We forget how many tools from our professional lives can help us systematically and thoughtfully work through problems and brainstorm solutions in our personal lives. Instead of just emoting at one another, Dr. Rosenthal counsels couples to place big decisions, like a move, out there as you would with colleagues at work: "Put it on the table, brainstorm, evaluate all the options without judging any of them negatively or shooting any of them down."

The process is important. "When people feel they were included in the decision, and they had time to really come to terms with it, even if it wasn't their top choice, they then often feel okay with the decision," she said.

I caught up with Kelsey a year after our first chat. Believe it or not, they had moved back to D.C. She launched her own legal recruiting firm with a new business partner. Scott secured a tenured position at a prestigious university.

The Texas they knew in 2015 wasn't the Texas they had been living in anymore. The laws and policies of the state had shifted deeply right. This not only impacted Scott's job because he worked for a public university, but they have two daughters now. They want them growing up under policies that align with their own political beliefs.

Kelsey approached Scott with the idea to move. This time, it was for all of them.

The process was long and slow. From first feeler to written offer, they waited 500 days. Jobs like Scott's are based on the hiring needs of the organization, so Kelsey had to plan for it to either happen or not happen. "My brain was running a million miles a minute for basically a year," she said. And even though she sacrificed for her husband's career all those years ago, it's starting to feel like her turn again. From where I sit, as her friend, I'm enjoying the view.

When you propose a big change that requires your partner to make a sacrifice, you should be able to identify a *why* that's bigger than money. Otherwise, their sacrifice may not be as worth it as you think.

During our conversation, Ashley shared a personal detail that struck me deeply. In 2003, she was eliminated in her senior year of military school due to the U.S. "Don't Ask Don't Tell" policy at the time. Most of her classmates went on to serve overseas—some of them never came home.

"As I sat in a cushy chair in an air-conditioned office, I had to reconcile that for years," she told us. "My entire career has just been about trying to earn it, and I will never earn it. I will never earn that grace, and I know that."

I think Jane realizes her and Ashley's ambitions need to be satisfied in different ways. Jane, on one hand, doesn't want the spotlight. She is a curious person who wants to do good work and be challenged.

Ashley's looking for something else. She calls it significance. I think it might be more.

Whatever it is, she's absolutely not after it alone.

22.
IN BETWEEN

Losing your job can feel like losing your power. As partners, we want to be fixers, but give them room before you step in.

Caleb saw it coming.
 Well, kind of. He saw it coming for so long that he didn't know how or when it would come.
 A main condition of the job Caleb started in January 2020 was that he'd relocate to Texas. The initial plan was to fly down weekly from New Jersey until he and his wife, Bailey, were certain the role was worth uprooting their family for. We all know what happened after that: lockdowns, remote work, *We're All In This Together*, Corporate America said.
 That is, until we weren't. Until push came to shove. Caleb had been working from home for three years when moving trickled back into the conversation with his bosses, who knew at this point

he didn't want to relocate. Not when he was proving how well the job could be done at home. A lot can change in three years: toddlers become children; privileges become ways of life; dealbreakers prove to be much less rigid than they once were, except for this one.

Caleb's position got eliminated. He was out of work, searching for a job.

There are more ways to lose your job now than ever before: mass layoffs, forced demotions, surprise probation, sudden buyouts, strategic reorgs, return to office mandates so unworkable they operate as stealth layoffs. At the end of the day, you're out of work. But some of the tactics organizations use to reduce their workforce muddy the line between personal and corporate responsibility, giving big things that are not within your control the appearance that they are through a micro-choice left up to you. These conscious un-couplings can feel just as unceremonious as the words, "You're fired," with the added confusion of whether losing your job was within your control or not.

Losing your job feels like losing your power. No matter how you end up there, dramatic swings in your income, time, or purpose can make anyone feel stripped of control over their daily life.

Yet, the worst tension might come from inside the house. You and your partner can have different ideas about searching for a new job—about what is *enough* and what can be done. About what temporary financial changes to make and what should get to stay the same. There can be blame, guilt, projection, angst, even in dual-income households with high standards of living, because remember, it's all relative. Almost no one is totally immune from feeling the pressure of real disturbances to real life.

Elizabeth Earnshaw, a licensed marriage and family therapist and author of *'Til Stress Do Us Part,* frames stress on relationships as **external** and **internal**. Losing your job is an external stress: an event that occurs outside of your relationship. But an external

22. IN BETWEEN

stress can place *internal* stress on both of you when you haven't shared enough information with each other, or you're struggling to communicate about a constructive path forward.

She cautions against offering solutions too fast when you should probably just be listening. "Especially when it comes to losing your job," she said, "the other partner can get so anxious that they almost seem demanding in a way that's going to be counterproductive."

I felt her point. Douglas and I have fallen into this pattern a lot over the years. I'd have a problem at work, and he'd provide some cavalier solution that would never fly in a corporate setting. Then, he'd have a tough client meeting, and I'd jump into lawyer-triage-mode, ready to play out every potential bad outcome. We probably both just needed a hug. Instead, we caused more stress and eroded our ability to collaborate, all because we wanted to fix things right then and there.

We all want to fix problems for the people we love, but there's an order of operations. You need to listen first to avoid belittling them and piling onto an already stressful situation.

Earnshaw believes this is about emotionally tuning in to your partner at a time when they might be feeling all sorts of things. Asking open-ended questions will clue you into what they need. "Let them know they have permission to not problem solve with you right away," she said. "They have permission to just be upset."

Caleb's job search stretched from weeks to months. Finding comparable work proved harder than expected, and it wasn't easy to just remain calm and carry on.

"Look, I'll be 100% honest," he said, turning to his wife during our interview. "For me, there was a little bit of like, the best word I can think of is embarrassment. I felt pressure that I was placing on you, which you weren't even giving me."

Bailey comes from a very different place than Caleb. Her family immigrated from Russia when she was a child. She watched her parents learn English, get jobs, thrive at work, build wonderful lives from nothing. To her, Caleb's job search was a challenge he could bootstrap himself through like any other. It was just a blip. Stay positive and persistent, and it will all work out.

That wasn't quite how he felt.

"I felt overwhelmed, just in terms of wanting to live up to expectations and be able to provide for the family," he admitted. "Not having the knowledge of what might come next or when something might come along, there were moments where I felt overwhelmed, and I would unload on her."

There's a familiar word again: *provide*.

Their whole lives, men are taught one meaning of that word: to provide is to earn money.

Bailey and Caleb have always earned around the same income, but losing his job felt like losing his purpose under a commonly held belief that it's a man's job to be a breadwinner for his household. That may sound like a conservative take, but even on a subconscious level, it's a cultural truism engrained throughout the United States and high-income countries in Europe.

Research indicates how men's unemployment can negatively impact heterosexual couples. They begin to struggle with self-respect and their job search becomes a feature of everyday life, placing pressure on the relationship to return to their culturally accepted norm as soon as possible.[49]

Of course, one of the goals of this book is to help you break free from rigid gender beliefs like this. Men, you can contribute to your family in other ways—and you should. You're much more than a paycheck to the people who love you.

To conquer the internal stress from an external event like losing your job, you both need to address head-on what transitions need to take place in your lives.

"In any life transition—you have a baby, you change job statuses, you move, somebody breaks a leg, whatever—you should always be

22. IN BETWEEN

talking about the changes in navigating roles and responsibilities," said Earnshaw. "If you don't talk about that, then you are likely to breed resentment, because what's going to happen is you'll maintain similar dynamics that don't make sense anymore."

There's no room for ego in this. If you're suddenly the spouse who is available more, you should assume more unpaid labor to relieve your partner's load. Offer support in ways you couldn't before. This does more than alleviate pressure from your partner, who might be the sole driver of your household income for the time being. You are actively broadening your role within your family. You are learning how much more you can offer.

While he was out of work, Bailey and Caleb let their childcare lapse. He assumed the primary role of caring for their seven and 10-year-old kids, and felt time turn to quicksand almost every day.

"You realize the day is not nine-to-five anymore," he said. "The kids leave at nine. Now, I need to get myself together, and by the time I do that, it's ten, and then I need to be back to pick them up by three. So, the day gets shortened from eight or nine hours to five at best. And then, if you throw in, you know, laundry a few times a week and grocery shopping and everything else, there are only so many hours you have to actually do any work, right?"

Right.

The juggle is real. Bailey and Caleb both acknowledged the stress he felt while balancing his job search with the kids' needs, but they wouldn't change it. "It gives you a different appreciation of time," she said.

During a period of unemployment, reevaluating roles isn't all you need to do. You may need to change how you're spending money, too.

For men, this is much harder to accept than having to pick up some extra carpools. In her interviews of 72 U.S. middle-class families in which one parent became unemployed, Aliya Hamid Rao uncovered a gendered correlation to how far parents will stretch to maintain their class status. Fathers sought to maintain their children's lifestyles as best they could, viewing their inability to do so as a personal failure. But when mothers fell unemployed, the families were more willing to cut back on personal expenditures without fear of losing their position in life.[50]

Again, I think these gendered distinctions have much to do with enduring cultural norms that are just very hard for people to break free from. It's no wonder the same men who are caught in their limited scope of what it means to provide for their families are hesitant to acknowledge any changes that need to occur in their family's spending during a period of unemployment. While driven by ego, perhaps, I don't view it as a character flaw. When you love people, you want to give them what they want. It can just be as simple as that.

"We try to protect people from discomfort a lot," Earnshaw said. "A lot of times the person who loses their position, maybe they don't want to talk about it, because they don't want anything to have to change."

Bailey and Caleb never told their kids that Caleb lost his job. It was a plausible plan, since he already worked from home.

"I didn't feel like I was lying to them, but it didn't feel good," he said. "I just didn't want to feel like I'm letting them down, and I didn't want them to feel let down if they saw their dad couldn't manage to find a freaking job after nine months."

They were fortunate, as they acknowledged, to be able to maintain their lifestyle with Bailey's income. But many working families have tough decisions to make. Skirting around them only compounds your problems, placing more internal stress on your relationship than the financial discomfort you're trying to avoid.

Spending less isn't the only financial strategy you can implement when one of you loses your job. Douglas tells almost everyone to prioritize trying to save **at least six months of your living expenses in cash** for tough times just like this. Cash reserves do

22. IN BETWEEN

more than preserve your family's lifestyle in times of transition—they give you a runway to sort things out without projecting your panic all over each other. In the meantime, maybe your partner dials back on retirement contributions to free up more short-term cash, if you need it.

There are ways to make this less painful on your wallet and each other. They all start with listening and end with controlling what you can.

You're right to realize you're not *in this together* with every employer who ever told you so. But you are in this together with your wife, your husband, your kids. You don't need to navigate this season alone.

23.
THE POWER OF EXPECTATIONS

With so much riding on who you are, who will be there when you become someone else?

Years ago, in one of my favorite online groups, a post by a fellow lawyer caught my eye. She had just summited Mt. Kilimanjaro—aptly, on International Women's Day. She wrote of her accomplishment as life-defining, for a moment, until she returned to her day job confined by the same standards and limitations she'd always faced.

She started the conversation in search of ways to reconcile her superhuman experience with her ordinary life. Though most of us had no direct point of comparison, we could relate. A mergers and acquisitions lawyer wrote that after dedicating months of her life to a monster deal, she feels lost once it closes. Some distance runners shared the sadness that washes over them after completing a marathon (there's a name for this: the post-marathon blues).

23. THE POWER OF EXPECTATIONS

Dedicating yourself to a massive goal can be intoxicating, but what follows the euphoria of reaching a peak?

Much of our struggle has to do with expectations. When you commit so much of yourself to accomplishing one excellent thing, the intensity requires an almost delusional level of confidence. Expectations become the benchmarks that keep you moving forward, but they add a lot of weight as you go.

When I was out on my first maternity leave, writing our first book in the middle of the night, I developed an unreasonable expectation of my own. I started to romanticize this idea that at 30 years old, I could write my way out of my career as a lawyer through a hit personal finance book. Mind you, we had zero network and no marketing plan beyond throwing the book into the sky like a carrier pigeon. We also didn't have any mentors to guide us with real information on the book publishing process. Still, I was just working so hard on this one big thing, I let my drive turn into expectations that carried me away.

One of the great dangers of high expectations is not meeting them. For every person reconciling their comedown from a major win, there are even more grappling with loss. They never reached the peak—at least not their idea of what it would look like. Therein lies the danger of conflating heightened expectations with objective measurements of success. You can be excellent and still not meet the expectations that you, or those around you, have set. Then what?

I spoke with Dr. Megan McCoy, a professor who you heard from earlier, about her research on the financial overconfidence of student athletes. Elite athletic training begets high levels of self-efficacy, which is your confidence to perform certain skills or tasks. However, self-efficacy doesn't always translate well in the outside world if someone's confidence far outweighs their actual knowledge on a topic like personal finance.[51] In a nutshell, your high expectations in one part of your life can cloud your judgment in another.

Our conversation turned to the idea of second acts—about pouring so much into something that you know will eventually end, perhaps not even on your own terms. Time and fate get to decide when some things end.

We began to reminisce. Dr. McCoy remembered crying on the field during Senior Night in high school. I remembered the curtain going down on my last piano concert. Even as teens, we both felt the grief of losing these central parts of our identities.

This happens to some married couples when their children grow up. "There's a big divorce pop when kids leave for college, and it's not just unhappiness," she said. "It's that you didn't have an identity outside of the kids."

All those years. All that time. All the expectations either met or not.

Disappointment looks for space closest to home.

If you've closed your partner off from a central piece of your identity, you'll have a hard time bringing them in when you're searching for a new one. But if they are your true teammate, the opposite will happen. They will galvanize your strength to move through uncertain times.

I'm about to offer you a great example of the role your partner can play in both managing expectations and seeing you through to your next act: couples who survived the National Football League.

We spoke with two of them. Tim Kohn played for the Oakland Raiders in the late Nineties and met his wife, Shannon, in college. So did Trey Burton, whose career as a former Florida Gator and Philadelphia Eagle gave Douglas and I much to geek out over. He met his wife, Yesenia, in Gainesville, Florida (which is where we met, too).

Professional athletes have loads of expectations placed on their backs. There's the coaches, analysts, fans, and frankly, their entire

23. THE POWER OF EXPECTATIONS

communities. Jorrell Bland, a financial advisor and former college player, specializes in helping athletes become financially literate and navigate their lives after the clock runs out. He told me, most people don't think about the person behind the athlete. They think about results.

"When you're dealing with those expectations of who you're supposed to be, especially for an athlete who has made it to the ultimate level, everybody—not only in their family but their school, their neighborhood—is like, *you did it, now we're expecting you to be great.*"

Having a spouse who can support the intensity of working towards these expectations is the ultimate power move. Both former players we spoke with played for several teams over several years. At times, they got paid week to week. They didn't know whether to rent or buy or surf on a teammate's couch. Their careers could fly to the moon or be over tomorrow, and their wives said, let's ride.

"I'll tell a lot of young guys that the woman you marry and have kids with can change the course of your life," Bland said. "It goes both ways, because if you pick somebody for the wrong reasons who does not uplift you, you're going to find yourself in a world of trouble when the things you were providing are no longer around."

Shannon Kohn and Yesenia Burton are not those women. They did more than roll with the punches. They infused their own sense of responsibility into their husband's careers, using strengths from their own backgrounds as a grounding force.

Tim gushed, "All the good stuff came from meeting Shannon in college, getting married, and having the family and life together that we have. Her influence really kept me from making some very arrogant and ill-conceived choices as a professional football player."

Shannon came from a small family of farmers in Iowa and knew how to work and how to save. When Tim's third-round signing bonus came through, they didn't change much from their frugal habits in college. "Being together under meager circumstances, we learned to enjoy ourselves," he said. "We didn't feel we had to impress each other by spending on this or that."

Not everyone was this way. "When you're with the NFL wives, there can be an arms race on extravagant spending," Shannon said of the jewels, vacations, and steakhouse dinners. "We knew what our priorities were. I think that was a big thing. We wanted financial security and to not be in a place where our hand was forced."

Trey and Yesenia led with trust, in the process and each other.

As a child of two independent business owners, Yesenia learned to help with her parents' books in high school and continued working in college until she and Trey got pregnant junior year. Living on food stamps and scholarship checks, times were tight, but they had a plan: play to their individual strengths. Do their respective jobs. One foot in front of the other, again and again.

"We have a very trusted independence in each of our things that kind of fuels us," she said.

Trey agreed. "The biggest blessing for me was that I never had to stress or worry about what was going on at home," he said. "She had a crash course in parenting and finances, but I had trust in all that she was doing. I knew that she could figure it out, so that gave me the freedom to go every single day and do whatever I could to grind it out and make as much as I could."

They knew that certain aspects of Trey's career would be out of their control, so they tempered those expectations and took each season—each week, for a time—as it came. From not getting drafted, to a $10,000 signing bonus with the Eagles, to a Super Bowl ring, to a $32 million contract with the Chicago Bears that terminated early due to injury, they rode the wave together.

Until it stopped. Everyone stops—it's just a matter of when.

Tim got cut four times in three years.

"After the first time, I had the epiphany that most players have either when they realize their career is very finite because they

23. THE POWER OF EXPECTATIONS

have limited talent, or when they realize that the clock is running out on them and their ability to just keep earning money," he told us. "So, when you start realizing money is a finite commodity, you start caring about your stewardship of it more."

The end of the road can be humbling. For some, it feels like a cliff.

"I've seen people become suicidal over it," said Bland, the financial advisor. "This was everything to them, and they feel like they've lost it, or they feel like they could've done more. So, having this support system of people who are going to tell you, listen, you're not just Jorrell Bland, The Football Player. You're Jorrell Bland. This is you. You still have so much more to give in other aspects of your life than putting on a uniform and your pads and your cleats."

This is about more than losing work. It's about reconstructing your identity, post-expectations.

When you're faced with redefining yourself, you can take it with you. Your tenacity for one thing can be your power for another if you extract the takeaways of what went well and what didn't. The same can be said for love. True resilience isn't about just surviving or giving the appearance that you're fine to anyone who's set expectations of you. It's about using your challenges as your lessons to grow stronger.

The Burtons used one word to describe their second act: consistent. They've never been this still.

On the Gulf Coast of Florida, Trey golfs and fishes and loves being present for their three children, who aren't babies anymore. Like Dad, they're getting into competitive sports, which makes things interesting.

"His football brain is trained in analysis," Yesenia said. He loves evaluating new business opportunities to invest in, but he knows from the game to take it slow and see everything.

He also knows his best teammate is right beside him.

24.
UNDER THE INFLUENCE

You have every right to question what your partner consumes online.

There is a woman who used to live rent-free in my mind. Instagram brought me to her as a supporting character of other Manhattan women I couldn't stop staring at.

Exorbitant wealth is hard to look away from, though maybe, my algorithm just cornered me in this space. I was glued to the trappings of a so-called lifestyle: the designer wares billed as "investment" pieces (though I wondered how one could have so many investments); the "simple" meals prepared by private chefs at backyard tables in the Hamptons; the birthday parties that likely cost more than our wedding. Jealousy isn't the entire reason—I understand we live on different socioeconomic planets—but me and the followers of women like these are clearly ogling at something.

24. UNDER THE INFLUENCE

Comparison is sneaky. So is social media. Whether you linger around the content you aspire to, or are even disturbed by, you will be fed more of it. Intrigue leads to insidious comparison—the kind you're hesitant to admit is happening. I once got caught in a cycle of TikToks about colorectal cancer in young people, and you better believe I stuck around to hear all their symptoms to make sure I've never had them.

With this one woman, it just seemed so charmed. So gauche. And yet, my brain played tricks, turning questions like, *how do they have enough money to do that*, into *how much money would we need to do that?*

It's not a knock on your values to admit you're susceptible to tools that were built to capture you. Reality is too easy to filter away, but no ruse lasts forever.

In the summer of 2024, her husband committed suicide, and their serious money problems came into public view: overwhelming business debts, an overleveraged home in the Hamptons, rented furniture in their massive city apartment.[52] I have no schadenfreude over the tragedy of watching innocent children lose their father all while the internet scrutinizes their mother (who scrubbed her account). But I also can't dismiss the role that social media plays in bolstering false appearances, influencing our judgment, and damaging our relationships.

Before the digital age, the people who could influence your life were likely limited to political and business leaders, community organizers, writers, and your close family and friends. The internet blew that wide open. Now, journalists aren't the only ones telling stories. We are exposed to a global cast of characters. Anyone can frame their online platforms however they want, particularly if people are listening.

The core concept of "influence" has always been the same: that people are listening. The room's just a lot bigger—and noisier—than ever before.

When it comes to money, social media has completely changed our consumer habits and expectations. According to a 2023 Bankrate survey, 48% of social media users make impulse purchases from what they see online, spending more than $71 billion that year.[53] This is due to the speed and ease at which users are presented with not just opportunities to buy, but opportunities to compare.

I could think of no one better to speak with on this topic than Chelsea Fagan, author and co-founder of The Financial Diet. She believes that spending has always been social, predicated on what we're exposed to and what feels normal to us. These days, we're just able to see much more.

"It used to be that only rich people could see the lifestyles and spending choices of other rich people. Now, you can be low income and constantly bombarded with the lifestyles and spending choices of people who earn ten times your income," she said. "The flattening effect of social media makes it so that you now expect you should be able to do those same things."

Pair social media's ability to intensify our lifestyle expectations with the rampant increase in scarcity marketing tactics and buy-now-pay-later services to see how we are enabled by design. Just as troubling as our spending behaviors is how we've normalized things that just... aren't normal. Let me ask you this:

- Should you be shooting the gender of your baby out of a T-shirt cannon?
- Should you spend time meticulously organizing your plasticware (or underwear) like a domestic game of Tetris?
- Should you be filming the mundanity of your morning skincare routine followed by your nonconsenting toddler's tantrum while you mix your iced matcha latte with a glass straw?

24. UNDER THE INFLUENCE

The internet says you can, and you should. By giving these performative acts our attention, we've come to accept a permanent state of "pics or it didn't happen." Everything is a chance to put your lifestyle on display or conform to those who do.

Think about the immense pressure this places on your loved ones. They may not even realize you're trying to live up to a manufactured standard you absorbed online. All they may see is you projecting that what you have together, behind the smartphone, isn't *enough*.

Influence is directly linked to consumption in this form. So, if your partner is overconsuming, you absolutely have the right to tell them. Fagan agrees.

"I think it's totally fair for a partner to say, I don't think watching this stuff is good for us—I really don't think we should have it in our media diet," she said. "The same power of pushback we should have on each other's financial choices, we should have on media consumption habits."

When the damaging message goes beyond chasing lifestyles, it gets even darker.

Too often, influencers push content underscored by social agendas priming you for relationships in which power is so imbalanced, they could pose a danger to your financial or physical health. I've called Douglas a Man In Finance in jest, but the notion of "optimizing yourself for a high-value man," as Fagan put it, is a cringeworthy diminution of your worth. Men face it, too, seeing online gym gurus conflate physical jackedness with self-improvement. Worst of all might be the "tradwives" and "SAHGs" (that's Stay-At-Home Girlfriends), who idealize their submissiveness as a noble goal for women, whether they're milking cows or spending their allowances at Cartier.

Make no mistake: any message that romanticizes handing all your agency over to your spouse is a dangerous one. These are the exact power dynamics that destroy relationships. They destroy people.

But most of us won't be going sober, no matter what form the internet shape shifts into next. The best you can do is tailor your consumption to curate who you listen to. Some pockets online can be incredibly supportive places to grow, learn, and think critically. And not all mechanisms for comparison are bad, either, if they help you validate that something happening in your life isn't okay.

"The way to use influence positively, I think, is to influence yourself to ask questions that are otherwise unasked," Fagan said. "Try to reframe the things that become engrained habits and norms, and use it to form community and connection that allows for a much more positive, healthy, egalitarian life."

25.
THE SIGNS

Money can be used to control you.

In this section, we showed you how money interacts with power and gave you constructive ways to rebalance that power, because underlying these concepts is a love worthy of criticism. A love worthy of improving.

But here's the bad part.

The dark side of power is control. People can use money to gain control over their partners.

Restricting your ability to acquire and access money is one of the most powerful methods of trapping you inside of a toxic or abusive relationship. Indeed, financial abuse occurs in nearly 99% of domestic violence cases,[54] but it can take many forms. It can be subtle and manipulative—even commingled with mental illness. It can be destructive and driven by addiction. It can be overt and obvious to everyone but you.

In any of these circumstances, you don't need to rebalance power. You just need to get out.

I can't provide you with an exhaustive list of all the warning signs of financial abuse, but I can lead you to the scent. As friends, family, or something less than that, we've all borne witness to circumstances that don't seem right. Sadly, I've learned with age that many of the bad things we think could be happening are actually happening, but that validation often comes too little and too late. This chapter is as much for those bearing witness. You could be a lifeline for someone in need.

It's just as hard to see when it's you.

Chaos was all that Amanda knew. She was a third-generation pregnant teenager, falling into a familiar pattern by marrying the father of her child. He was the life of the party, and he sucked the life out of her.

"What's most scary to me now is that I never felt unsafe, and I absolutely should have," she admitted. "I was like the frog in boiling water who doesn't know she's boiling until she's dead."

I will share only glimpses of Amanda's story with you, because I don't want you locked into one version of what this looks like. Women get abused. Men get abused, too. Some things that happened to Amanda were textbook financial abuse. But at a point, her ex-husband fell deep into addiction, which he ultimately perished from. I think it's near impossible for anyone to draw clean lines around what drove his behavior and when. Maybe for once in this whole book, it's about the signs much more than the story.

I spoke with Dr. Jamie Zuckerman, a licensed clinical psychologist and narcissistic abuse expert, about how abusive relationships begin.

"It feels like a tidal wave," she said, like you're being swept into a fairytale. "If you hear things about being their soulmate, or making future plans together, or talking about your future kids' names when you're three dates in, I tell people to run."

The vulnerable details you get lured into sharing will serve a purpose for them later. "What that person's doing is making it seem like they really get you so that you unload on them, and then down the road in the relationship, they hold that information against you."

25. THE SIGNS

Then comes trying to control you through money. Dr. Zuckerman called the tactics a "spider web," which follow a predictable pattern, but that pattern is hard to see when you're being gaslit about everything. "You come to believe you're not capable of seeing reality correctly, and you are therefore not capable of making good decisions."

In Part Two, I asked how your partner talks about your mistakes. Let's bring that full circle. If he's latching onto a small bump in the road from years ago to convince you that in the present, you are incapable of handling any aspect of your finances, he's trying to manipulate you. He may frame it as trying to protect you. He may mask it as a chivalrous gesture to alleviate you, his queen, of the burdens of something as pedestrian as money.

None of that is real. You don't need protecting. This goes not only for women, but men who have been diminished into their own paralysis.

Financial control and abuse may look like:

- Limiting your access to accounts and passwords
- Scrutinizing your receipts and expenses
- Impeding or sabotaging your ability to work and earn money
- Withholding money for arbitrary reasons
- Making major purchases without your consent
- Opening lines of credit in your name
- Removing one of your names from jointly owned assets
- Demanding sex in exchange for money

From the start, Amanda's ex latched onto her insecurities. He knew she was young, and passive, and would do what he said.

She stayed home when their first child arrived and became

responsible for helping him find (and keep) a job. She realizes now, "I was doing a lot of the things that made him look so great." She filled out his applications, completed his aptitude tests, and even proofread emails at his beck and call during his workday. The better work he got, the more insecure he grew. When his mother died, his substance abuse took hold.

In their case, Amanda paid the bills. But even before he was siphoning their money for drugs, he had little regard for her input. They'd be on their last dollar, and he'd spend it how he pleased. At one point, he realized it was better to let Amanda work, so he could take her money, too. But he hated sharing her. He hated seeing her befriend colleagues, dress nicer, do anything that made her feel good about herself. So, he sabotaged her right out of her great corporate job, applying so much physical and emotional pressure that she crumbled.

"When you're in this cycle, it's almost like you're addicted to this person, because they make you think no one's ever going to want you," Amanda told me. "It's like they become this faulty mirror, and they're reflecting this really ugly image back to you, and you believe it."

Dr. Zuckerman specializes in helping couples navigate the complexities of narcissistic behavior. She has seen how dark things can get.

I asked her, to be sure, where love exists between an abuser and a victim. Does it? Can it?

"The ultimate goal of power in these relationships is to literally take ownership and control over your sense of self until you're a shell," she replied. "Once you're empty and can't give any more, they discard you for someone else."

This is what happened to Amanda. They were about to be evicted from their mobile home when her ex left for California. He said he'd send for them, but she knew better, and their finances told the truth. He removed his name from the car lease she co-

25. THE SIGNS

signed. He wiped out their joint bank account. He stole her credit cards and maxed them out, too.

"It was terrifying," she said. "There was no back-up, no rainy-day fund, there was nothing."

To settle up, Amanda sold all their furniture. She packed her kids into the truck and drove them in a terrible snowstorm to stay with her mother. This was the beginning of the end—an end that took a long time and cost them a lot. Hell, it cost the children their father. But after sitting with their story, I have to acknowledge the one true blessing: she didn't have to escape.

If you or someone you love needs to remove themselves from an abusive relationship, tread carefully at first, suggests Shweta Lawande, a CFP® professional. "You can expect the worst from a financially abusive man who feels like he's been pushed into a corner," she said.

The best thing you can do is equip yourself with as much money and information about your financial situation as possible before sending any signals. This includes collecting receipts, account statements (even photographing the hard copies if you must), and any evidence of financial or physical abuse. Keep it somewhere safe, perhaps with a friend. Open a new bank account at a different bank and start stashing money bit by bit. Depending on how tightly your partner reviews your receipts, you may also try buying gift cards in small amounts at the grocery store or pharmacy.

Recognize that "leaving" is a process. Depending on your personal financial resources, how financially enmeshed you are with your abuser, and whether you have children together, you will have different steps to take.

A financial advisor can help you quarterback all the professionals you'll need to repair your life. At her firm, Lawande has pulled in financial therapists, credit specialists, family lawyers, and even private investigators. It's a team effort, and the team should be talking. If you're concerned about cost, there are still resources available to you. For example, Savvy Ladies® is a non-profit organization that offers free financial education for women, as well as a financial helpline you can call with questions for an advisor.[55]

Power is a tool I wish was only used for good, but I can't wish away the truth.

Whether you are finding your power, using your power, or assessing who or what has power over you, you will need one thing: courage.

YOUR QUESTIONS ON POWER

1. Do you feel powerful in your relationship?
2. What are your goals for the next three years?
3. How important is your career to you?
4. Have you made any sacrifices for your partner's career?
5. Who sets the highest expectations of you?
6. Are you consuming anything online that doesn't serve you?
7. Are you in control of your money?
8. Do you have access to all your accounts and statements?
9. Do you feel free to work?
10. Do you feel free to spend?

PART V.
RISK

We revisited the past. We dug deep into the present. Finally, we look forward.

Your goal in understanding risk is to prepare for a spectrum of possibilities. You are the risk managers of your own relationship, which means you can account for all your feelings and facts to make authentic choices that lessen the chances of your fears coming true.

Financial outcomes are never certain. However, learning to prepare as a couple can make you elastic for when the unexpected happens. We will show you there are many paths to what you want, and there are a million ways back home.

You will find a few more examples of teamwork and the roles you play in helping your partner take big swings. You might be an integral part of protecting their downside. That doesn't mean you need to get lost in the process.

In the end, we leave a silent trail that touches everyone we love. That is our legacy—our biggest opportunity of all.

26.
THE RIDE

You are the risk managers of your own lives.

One year for my birthday, Douglas had a surprise for me. The guy's not big on surprises, but he seemed very proud of whatever he had planned. I assumed we'd be seeing a Broadway show or spending the day at a spa (both are treats that help me level set when I'm feeling a little lost). But nope. As he drove us south on a New Jersey highway, I was perplexed right up until I saw the sign. He hit the turn and said to me, "You've got to let go."

He took me to Six Flags Great Adventure, the theme park with the largest roller coasters in the state. This was neither the cultural nor Zen experience I was looking for. But in his defense, it held sentimental value. We used to live for the days of piling into our friends' cars to ride coasters around Florida. We still love the suspense. The thrill. Your body perceives it's in danger, while your brain knows that aside from some freak occurrence out of a *Final Destination* movie, you'll be just fine. You can be uncomfortable without being unsafe. You can enjoy the ride.

Risk was one of the earliest concepts that ever clicked for

me, even as a young lawyer with little desire to take risks of my own. I spent more than a decade in the commercial insurance industry, observing the way organizations assessed tough choices they faced. I mapped out decision trees for stakeholders. I saw how little decisions can have big consequences when you're not viewing risk through a wide enough scope, or with a long enough runway. Most relevant for our purposes, I learned a hell of a lot about compromise.

I believe people are risk averse, because they are thinking in terms that are too binary. You're either putting it all on black, or you're not playing the game. You're jumping out of planes, or you'll never get to fly.

Couched in sarcasm, I bet you've heard this question before: *What's the worst that can happen?*

But let me ask you for real. What are your worst-case financial, professional, physical, and emotional scenarios?

These are the outer limits of what you could face as a couple.

Now, what are you willing to avoid, omit, save, or pay, to offset the chances of those scenarios happening?

Risk deals with chances—not just choices. Even if you're terrified of your worst-case scenario and want to do everything in your power to prevent it, you still might not be able to. That's why fear and avoidance are so harmful: you end up blind to the possibility of all outcomes. You lose opportunities to shoot for the good and plan for the less-than-good. For example, a lot of families purchase life insurance policies but never consider the lesser event of falling ill, being unable to work, and not earning their full salaries for an extended period of time.[56] These things happen, too.

My point is that the risks we encounter every day require dynamic thinking. We can't mitigate them in black and white—they exist on a sliding scale of importance and consequence. They are less like a leap of faith and more like a roller coaster: attached to our realities but filled with drama, nonetheless.

26. THE RIDE

You are the risk managers of your own relationship.
I promise, you can understand risk better. The sooner you do, the sounder your judgment will be. When things don't go as planned—and you know they won't always—you can take solace in the fact that you considered it could happen. You envisioned it. Planned for it. The alternatives didn't catch you by surprise, sending you and your partner into freefall.

Seatbelts on.

Your *risk appetite* is how you feel about taking on risk. It's a sentiment personal to you.

In one study, researchers set out to differentiate the personality traits of positive and negative risk-takers, but they ended up identifying some psychological factors for risk-taking in general. Whether you're putting yourself out there with a new friendship (a positive risk) or binge drinking (a negative risk), both stem from factors like your sensitivity to punishment; your tolerance for uncertainty; your perspective about your future; and your sensitivity to reward.[57]

We started this book by telling you that your story is your story. When it comes to love and money, your past informs the person you are today. Let's bring that concept back around.

The things you've seen and experienced—wins, wars, recessions, traumas—cultivate your optimism or cynicism for how things will turn out in the future. Both partners' feelings about a certain risk can only be understood when you're curious enough to learn what got you here. In other words, everything *up to here* helps you understand everything *you do from here*.

Your risk appetite can also change. When I first met Douglas, he had a bottomless hunger for risk. As the son and grandson of serial entrepreneurs, he grew up in an environment where problems arose and then got solved. He was handed the tools to fix things himself—an invaluable skill I always admired—but that caused him to not think much about the consequences of his words or actions.

Though I guess, at the time, there weren't many, which is a perfect segue to my next point.

Your *risk capacity* is how much risk you can actually handle. While your feelings about risk are personal, couples should assess their capacity to take on risk together.

Here's a basic but classic example of how risk capacity works in investing. When you're young, you have a greater incentive to take aggressive investment positions, because you likely have decades of market cycles ahead of you to regain any losses you incur. But you wouldn't "put it all on black" when you're three years away from a retirement goal that you've been saving your whole careers for. As you approach that money milestone, the last thing you'd want to do is allow your worst-case scenario to happen. Your risk capacity is at an all-time low.

In his twenties, Douglas's appetite and capacity for risk converged to unleash a feral Frankendoug on New York City. He was willing to try anything to make a name for himself in the financial services industry and truly didn't care what a single person thought about it. He strolled into red carpet events like he belonged there. He spammed financial journalists. He sent manilla-envelope-sized mailers congratulating hundreds of lawyers around the city for making partner at their firms. He did this, because what was the worst that could happen? He was a young, childless man with a paycheck and a sublease. His worst-case scenario was going home.

At the time, I came from such a different place. With so much student loan debt and such poor job prospects, I felt like my appetite and capacity for risk were at rock bottom. I was *so emotional* about spending money, it was as if I didn't trust myself anymore. For Douglas, even though he didn't have much, he was never afraid to bet on himself with what little he had.

How you spend (or don't) says a lot about how you view risk.

We spoke with Dr. Scott Rick, an associate professor at the University of Michigan, who studies consumer decision-making.

26. THE RIDE

His book, *Tightwads and Spendthrifts*, builds on his original research to help couples understand why they approach spending the way they do. Dr. Rick's "tightwad-spendthrift scale" lets people know where they fall: if they are a *tightwad*, i.e., "someone who's very anxious about spending and spends less than they think they should," or a *spendthrift*, i.e., "someone with the opposite problem who spends more than they think they should." Many people fall in the middle. But across the scale, spending is hard for couples to talk about.

Interestingly, Dr. Rick told us that mixed tightwad-spendthrift couples probably have the most productive conversations about money. Two spendthrifts are all about avoiding reality until things bubble over. "Meanwhile, a dual tightwad house is peaceful, but they also seem a little boring. They rate very highly on measures of living a serene and uneventful life," he said.

As you've read, there's many reasons couples can't talk about money. Worry is a big one, which Dr. Rick explained: "We worry about abandoning our future selves and hurting that version of ourselves. We worry about missing out on the fun of life, and there's no right answer, so you can go around in circles forever. There's just so much uncertainty about what the future will look like—it's just very understandable that it would be such a mental minefield."

To his point, risk exists not only in what you do but in what you don't. Missed opportunities are harder to quantify, making risk even harder to justify to someone you love. I'll show you.

Years ago, a professor paired Lisa and Connor together on their first night of class. They'd be partners all semester, whether they liked it or not. Lisa was a commuting grad student, and Connor was on an adventure, soaking up everything New York City had to offer. On each group assignment, she'd do her part and then wait nervously for him to submit his portion mere hours before the deadline.

"Connor makes sure we tell people that we always got A's on those assignments," she grinned.

The next semester came, and Lisa asked herself whether she could stay paired with someone who worked so differently than she did: "Do I stay with the person who I know gets A's, even if they're not going to be super ahead of the deadlines, or do I try my luck elsewhere?"

She didn't realize how much that answer would impact her life. They've been together ever since, and they are still complete opposites in the ways they view risk.

Lisa is an only child who, like me, was taught to play it safe.

"I come from a family background predominantly focused on avoiding debt," she said. "So, a lot of the lessons I learned were around living within your means and paying cash whenever possible so as to not find yourself overly burdened by credit card statements that you're not able to account for down the line."

She wasn't exposed to the concept of using money to make money. That requires risk.

"One thing that's very important to me is not to be a burden," she said.

Lisa used the word *burden* enough to take notice. I understood that feeling. That's an only child feeling: to not know when you should care for others and when they should be caring for you. She carried her burden of moral responsibility into adulthood, making choices that align with what's safe and the least indulgent: she lived at home until she and Connor moved in together. For 11 years, she worked as a tenured teacher with guaranteed healthcare and a pension. She doesn't like credit. She *really* doesn't like spending money on things she thinks she could go without.

To her, money is best spent to lessen uncertainty—not to improve your quality of life.

For example, Lisa would use their growing cash reserves to repair a roof before it leaks. She would resurface their driveway before it crumbles. But she wouldn't put their money to work in an index fund or a high-yield savings account.

"That's probably the biggest difference between us," Connor said. "I guess I'm very comfortable being uncomfortable."

Now, about Connor. He and his twin brother grew up in public housing. They lived off food stamps. His mother never worked, and his father was incarcerated. But he overcame his challenges and broke free from the mold.

"When I think about risks and the choices we make around our finances, I feel like there's always this thing in the back of my head where no matter what happens, I survived that," he said. "So, like, what's $5,000? Let's take a gamble and invest in something, or let's buy something, because at the end of the day, money's just money. It comes and it goes."

Lisa has no student loan debt, but Connor had no choice. Without taking the financial risks to pursue his higher education—including a Ph.D. *after* their grad school program—he'd not have the earning power he has now. Connor leads a team in data science and AI for a publicly traded tech company.

To him, money is best spent investing in the life you want. Risk paves the way to that life.

Lisa is not convinced, though the train has clearly pulled out of the station.

Two years ago, Lisa left the safety of her classroom to join an education tech startup. When I asked how she came to terms with a career move that seemed out of character for her, she gave a robust explanation about bureaucracy and the teacher's union. I'm sure it's all true, but I heard Connor's explanation the loudest: he really wanted her to.

Connor earns the lion's share of their income. At one point, they saved up nearly three years of cash reserves. He works remotely. They don't plan on having children. The only thing that tied them to their starter home in a sleepy suburb was Lisa's job—and her discomfort. He knew how much they'd enjoy the freedom of remote work and a new home in a community that better fit their lifestyle.

"I would rather shoulder the burden of the finances to enjoy my life and my experiences versus having to accommodate her aversion to feeling like a burden," he said.

As a couple, their *capacity* for risk was quite high, but they needed to come together on their *appetites* for risk. I'd like to think I understand these things well, but we found someone much better to help us think it through.

Annie Duke is an author, decision strategist, and a champion of the World Series of Poker. She explained to me that we are most loss averse when we're thinking about switching things up. So, even if you hate your job, you're worried the next one will be even worse, so that keeps you from leaving even if the thing you're afraid of (being unhappy) is already taking place.

People also have a hard time recognizing when their capacity for risk has changed. "We habituate to whatever circumstances we are in, even when we hit the target," she said.

Duke suggests that instead of placing pressure on what to change right now, couples should look to the future and set criteria to act upon when certain goals are met: "When we do mental time travel, we tend to be much more rational about that future version of ourselves than we are about our present selves."

For example, someone in Connor's shoes could ask their spouse: *What would the circumstances need to be for you to feel comfortable leaving public education?*

Then to get there, Duke says, you need to cast yourselves forward once more. *What are the signs that you're doing what you need to do to get there? Are there behaviors you need to change?*

Some people have to brute force themselves into better risk management practices, like setting up automatic savings withdrawals or drawing extra hard lines in the sand. Others might realize they're much closer than they thought.

26. THE RIDE

In the case of Lisa and Connor, I could tell it took a lot for them to reach this new place they're in. Even with the means to do it, leaving her stable career and upgrading their lifestyle goes against most of what Lisa's known and accepted. She's no pushover, either; I think she just knew that for Connor, she had to try.

The best compromises leave everyone a little uncomfortable.

Risk is inherently uncomfortable, especially when you're agreeing to decisions you might have never made on your own. But sitting in the discomfort of healthy compromise is a skill everyone can benefit from. In a relationship, it means you're pushing each other in pursuit of something that matters to one of you more than the other. That agreement is a beautiful thing. It is a gesture that says: *I may not have chosen this, but I trust you. I am committed to the ride we are on.*

However, fair negotiations require information and lots of it. You need to know about your *capacity* to take on a certain risk, which is why in Part Four, we stressed the importance of stepping into your power with money. You should never lose control of your financial, emotional, or physical well-being to satiate your partner's appetite for risk. That would not be the result of a fair negotiation. That is your partner pushing you from the plane without teaching you how to use the chute.

When you're working with a financial professional, I share in Duke's opinion about keeping *your* opinions close to the chest on these matters. You don't want your feelings to predestine the advice. Rather, you can request three suggestions that are conservative, average, and less conservative. Evaluate them privately. See how they feel.

Where the line is, only you both know. Doing the work in this book will help you find out. When you take calculated risks together, the rewards are sweeter together. The losses hurt less, too.

Think about it for a moment. You would never wish to eliminate all risk if it meant forfeiting possibility. That is what we live for.

27.
NO CEILINGS

Business is personal when you're trying to build a life.

Relationships are a constant, at least in theory. There's a certain emotional safety and security in knowing the people who will stand beside you through thick and thin. Yet, intimately loving someone raises the stakes. It complicates decisions. The love between you and your partner serves as a constant reminder that the world is not only bigger than you but bigger than anything you might be building.

It's no easy task to love someone and love something—an idea, a business, a dream of your life's work. Whether you're buying a franchise or breaking ground on something with no template at all, you are inherently welcoming more variables into both of your lives.

An *Entrepreneur* article posed some valid reasons why a strong marriage can help entrepreneurs succeed. To name a few: you practice your communication skills often; you have to plan ahead; you work on compromise; you learn to stomach constructive

27. NO CEILINGS

criticism (again, in theory).[58] We observed the positive influence play out in many of the couples we interviewed.

Travis, for example, credits his wife Brianna for pushing him to start his accessible youth basketball program. "I really don't know what I would've done without her—she's the reason I did it," he said. Brianna's background in special education shapes the program, which uses methods of learning that are missing in youth sports. Travis and the business benefit from her influence. She acts as *his* coach: workshopping drills, troubleshooting facilities logistics, cheering on his dream while assuaging his fears of the unknown. He is awesome, but she's the special sauce.

I can attest to what I've seen at home, too. In the years since he's become a husband and father, Douglas is no longer the Frankendoug who moves fast and breaks things. He's been tempered by the purpose of building with us in mind. I am sure we could find instances where he's said no to opportunities that might have turned out great, but his healthier practices are a net positive for the business and us all.

Still, being married to an entrepreneur comes with its own set of trials.

Dr. Julie Gurner is a psychologist and an executive performance coach whose writing makes me feel like I can run through a brick wall. She told me, if there's any cracks in your relationship, nothing will bring those to the surface more than financial and business uncertainty.

In many ways for entrepreneurs, uncertainty is the baseline, but "the uncertainty itself can't be an obstacle," she said. Beyond the choppy waters of those relentless early decisions lies a sea of unexpected challenges that may calm over time but never cease. "You both have to see the uncertainty as opportunities."

You might recall Advika and Emanuel from Part One on *Beginnings*. They are both founders who have built venture-backed consumer companies. They didn't start their businesses at the same time, but they both know what it feels like to *not* know what will happen.

"I think we're both constantly six months away from running out of a job, right?" Advika laughed to her husband. She once went three years without paying herself. He's gone eight months.

"I would say more than that," he responded. "As founders, we're six months away from calling time on the thing that has taken a lot of energy in our lives and having to tell people you have to shut down because either the market didn't cooperate, or the decisions you took as a leader didn't work, or you ran out of money."

Financials aside, they know they are blessed to go through it together. Most couples can't stand in each other's shoes in this way.

"We are very lucky," Emanuel told me. "There are not many people who intimately understand what it's like to be in the role of the other person. So, when things aren't working out for me, she understands where I am, not just as my partner but as someone who's been through a lot of the things I'm experiencing currently."

Dr. Gurner spoke with me about who entrepreneurs are as humans. They are motivated, persistent, and have a lot of self-belief. Because of their tolerance for uncertainty, they may not really track with other people in their peer circles. This can be hard for a spouse to handle, being the comparative creatures we are.

When you're building, you may not be able to afford that new home or the holiday vacations. Your friends may roll their eyes when you decline big dinners or mute the group chats. It's hard to explain to others, even though you shouldn't care what anyone else thinks. But when you and your partner aren't both committed to the cause (and even sometimes, when you are), that social pressure can easily be weaponized against what you set out to accomplish.

Emanuel said it well: "It's like trying to bring something into the world that the world resists."

I know he meant from a business standpoint, but I also think

27. NO CEILINGS

resistance from the people closest to us hurts the most. Even with the utmost faith in you as a person, your friends and loved ones may just not understand.

"It's a lonely life, and it's not just like, *heavy is the head the wears the crown*," explained Matt Higgins, serial investor and author of *Burn the Boats*. "It's that you spend your days toiling on the bleeding edge, and the bigger the dream, the less people will be alongside you on that journey. Most people are inherently afraid of taking risks, most people conform, so if you're an entrepreneur, you know you're spending your days on the bleeding edge and there's nobody around to console you."

You can see this at all ends of the scale. My interview with a financial advisor for this chapter turned a bit meta. Samuel Deane bounced his baby girl on his knee while we spoke. He advises entrepreneurs but is also one himself. While still living at home, he didn't tell his dad for a *whole year* that he'd left his job to start his own practice.

"I would wake up in the morning, put on my suit, go to the gym, then he would leave for work, and I'd come home and start emailing clients, trying to do the things I needed to do to build my business," he said. Deane's parents left everything they knew to build a new life in America—and yet, to them, that wasn't as risky as Deane doing what he did. *Parents, man.* We share this in common. No one wanted me to leave my cushy corporate gig to chat with strangers about money.

Schisms like this make an entrepreneur's world even lonelier. Deane pointed out that many first-generation wealth builders have few resources they can rely on to know things like when to hire a CFO, how to allocate fundraised resources, or when to prioritize your family over continuing to invest your time in the business. There's just no blueprint. People also don't get that having flexibility doesn't mean you're available; in fact, you're probably working more than ever before. Only when Deane's wife opened her own Pilates studio did he feel like she was beginning to comprehend what he faced on a day-to-day basis. Now, she too knows how little separation exists between the "personal you" and the "you" building a business.

When we're feeling isolated, I think, we turn inward. Lacking relatable peers, loved ones, and resources can lead an entrepreneur to develop some real main character energy and start to believe what they're working on is The Most Important Thing In The World™. You could also, I guess, just be a complete narcissist. We observed some of that, too. Some "entrepreneurs" just never want to answer to anyone. They're in it for themselves, and that won't fare well in their business or personal lives.

"When entrepreneurial ventures are taken properly, it's a joint venture in which you're both playing different roles," Dr. Gurner said. "It isn't just everyone sacrificing for your needs."

As an entrepreneur, you must acknowledge the shared sacrifice taking place in your relationship. Think back to Part Four's chapter on power couples: an investment in one thing is a sacrifice in another. This admission is a sticking point for some. They don't want to acknowledge all their partners give for them to reach their goals.

Douglas was interesting when it came to this. He *overacknowledged* my role in his business. An expert in this book once told me he was the only male guest on her podcast to talk so much about his wife! As nice as that was, he also failed to recognize that what I gave him came at a cost.

Managing my job, the girls, and him, ran me ragged. I shed tears over *his* business opportunities, *his* emails, *his* brand. We crossed the line all the time. When I examine it now, I can hear his fear talking. After buying our home, building a family, and feeling the impact of his own parents' painful divorce, a lot of his spirit drained away. He didn't want to fail us, and he needed me.

27. NO CEILINGS

But I was giving him all the moments when I was ready to create moments of my own.

"It's not the dream of one partner to sacrifice in perpetuity and never have their own dreams met," Dr. Gurner said. "There has to be a real sense of reciprocity."

Douglas would tell you he doesn't regret how he's grown our business, except for any negative impact it's had on me or the kids. This is the truth. Because when you look back, most anything you view as a mistake won't be funding that fell through or a strategy that didn't pan out. It'll be the way you've treated the people you love.

For a moment, Advika grew quiet. Her father passed away from Covid-19. In four days, he was gone. She admitted, the one regret she has in building her company was prioritizing work over visiting him more in India. Now, Emanuel's mom is battling stage four ovarian cancer in East Africa. "I just keep saying to him, babe, go spend time with her," she said. "Being on the flip side of having lost a parent, I'm like, do it... you can't reverse some of the sacrifices you make."

There's the weight of it all, pressing on you from all sides.

"When you start a company, you're basically saying, 'I'm going to put this as a priority above all else,'" Advika said. "That is a hard commitment to back off from. Once you've taken venture funding, you've taken your friends' and family's money, you've put your own money into it, you're like, fuck, I can't fuck this up."

I wondered about the role that boundaries play in helping entrepreneurs find some peace with their loved ones. But as Dr. Gurner reminded me, you can't place terms like "boundaries" on this kind of work. Very rarely can someone tap out from building a business. "You're going to have periods of intensity," she said. "Those have to be understood by both parties."

Instead, commit to certain immovable priorities with your spouse. Discuss what makes each of you feel cared for. Maybe it's working out together or watching *House of Dragons* on Sunday nights. You could have a "phone free zone" when everyone's home for dinner. Another suggestion that benefits more of the people you love: don't ever miss a holiday. When you commit to these immovable priorities, you allow your marriage to improve your business by forcing a non-negotiable element of relational self-care into your life.

"Your partner becomes your scaffolding for those terribly lonely days when you know nothing is going right, but you know that at the end of the day you'd be perfectly fine with the life you have instead of the life you're trying to create," Matt Higgins said.

But yes, it's still hard. Beyond your commitments to everyone else is your commitment to yourself. Founders like Advika and Emanuel aren't in the game to just move fast and break things. They care about what they create. They share a purpose-driven ambition. They know there is no floor to what they do, but there's no ceiling, either.

I asked if they have enough.

Advika's spending time with her extended family. She loves her puppies (and Emanuel, of course). But no, it's not enough.

"I just don't think I'm a person who can be satiated," she said. "I don't know what will be enough. I'd like to say I'll know when we're there, but I don't know that we'll ever get there."

Emanuel is content with his material things. He says his health could use some work. But the goal he concedes neither of them have reached is the ball some entrepreneurs chase forever: impact.

No floors. No ceilings.

28.
LIVIN' ON THE HEDGE

Your best safety net might be standing right beside you.

What a difference four months can make.

In January 2024, we sat down with Tamara and Andy, friends of ours who started working together the year before. Andy had purchased a local optometry practice with the intent of modernizing the business and becoming *the* eye doctor for our community. Tamara has always been his boots on the ground. She brings her confidence to the business as much as her branding and management skills. She knows if this goes well, it can set them up for good.

"The amount of passion for wanting my family to succeed is something I'll never have at a company," she told me. "I can't imagine I would give that up."

We have a lot in common. Tamara and I both understand our personal skillsets well. We're energized by the prospect of elevating our family businesses. I get the sense that as mothers, we both feel like we've got something to prove, and we don't really know how or when that will stop.

But we bought into these *work-life* salads with our husbands under different circumstances, which matter in ways you'll find out in a minute. For now, know that we both demonstrate a universally important concept for couples learning how to manage risk: The Hedge.

A hedge is "something that protects you from a downside outcome," explained decision strategist Annie Duke. However, it always comes at a cost.

Duke and I talked through some examples. First, let's say, you want to have an outdoor wedding. You should try to reserve a venue with an indoor option, as a hedge against rain. Of course, you will pay more for that venue, but that's the price of protecting your downside.

Let's do another. You have a very important flight to catch—I mean, you cannot even consider the possibility of missing this flight. So, you arrive at the airport three hours early as a hedge against that happening. The cost? A $22 sandwich and two hours of your life sitting in a chair.

These are simple tradeoffs. You're able to see and feel the comfort of having a Plan B and extra padding in your schedule. But when it comes to the Big Picture Stuff, like your careers and your money landscape as a couple, the forecast is cloudier, because you can't predict every single bad outcome you'd want to hedge against. We can try by examining the probabilities of different scenarios, but we will never know it all.

Cash is the best hedge against the unknown. However, Duke says people have a tough time saving—and more so, a tough time figuring out the hedges they need against certain risks—because of two cognitive phenomena: *optimism bias* and *temporal discounting*.

Optimism bias is what it sounds like: people tend to believe everything will just work out. That sounds nice, but by not

28. LIVIN' ON THE HEDGE

considering the downside outcomes well enough, we're not calibrating the probabilities correctly, Duke said. I think it's an easy mindset for couples in business together to adopt, because we really want it to work out.

Pair that with temporal discounting, which "is that we will take a discount to get something now as opposed to waiting for it in the future." In other words, we are impatient. We'd rather accept a less optimal version sooner than plan, wait, and hedge our risks appropriately.

Andy admitted he wasn't comfortable with Tamara leaving her corporate job to come work with him when she did. He wanted the practice up, running, and stable first.

"I was trying to push her off," he said. "But she kept saying, 'I need to start now, so that we can get things going in the right direction. Our bet is that we're going to do this long term, why not make the most of it early on?'"

Tamara came in hot. She wanted to make staff changes, process changes, inventory changes, *all the changes*. "I'm a quick decision-maker," she told us. "I get on a path, and he wants me to pause, like, so many times."

They know they are different in this regard. Andy is methodical and careful. Tamara wants it now.

Renovations of their front optical store, for example, would cost $100,000. When we spoke that January, Tamara was ready to green-light the project, but Andy wanted to wait until they could purchase the building (an option of their buyout agreement), build back their emergency fund, and start taking some money out of the business to support their lifestyle again.

They were running lean.

"I want our business account to have enough of a cushion where something could happen tomorrow," Andy said. "I want to know we have that security and that we can start pulling money out for ourselves. Like, what can we put in our retirement plans? The 529 plans? All that stuff is not coming from anywhere else besides what we're doing right now."

But through his concerns shined respect for her. He values her opinion.

"You're very convincing," he smiled at her, "just again, the right decision and the right timing are two different things."

Sarah Behr is a financial planner who serves many clients in the start-up space. She's used to showing people how to hedge against risk.

"I probably wouldn't advise someone to go to a startup or change their life on the unknown unless I thought they could sustain it," she said. "Some of that depends on their situation."

For a long time, Douglas and I used my corporate salary and benefits as a hedge against the risks of growing and stabilizing his practice. This wasn't a choice at first: we had our student loan debt, a mortgage, two cars, and two preschool tuitions to pay for in a high-cost-of-living suburb we chose for its proximity to the city. But in the six years from when he founded the firm to when I joined full-time, we worked to save almost a year-and-half's worth of our living expenses in cash, while contributing to our retirements and the girls' 529 plans. I'm not telling you this to flex. I'm telling you this because running a business means more unknowns, more unexpected expenses, more chances for things to go wrong. When you're businessowners, more is more.

The stakes are also higher when you work with your partner. Life and money and work bleed together as one, such that there is no such thing as *just business*. We'd never pretend it's easy. The fights sting harder, but the wins are epic—more is more. I think the reason we're able to overcome many of the pain points of running a business together is because of the financial position we reached before jumping four feet in.

Behr and I discussed cash—as well as your partner holding down a steady income—as ways to mitigate risk when you're starting a

28. LIVIN' ON THE HEDGE

venture. But the same advice follows for taking on risks in lifestyle, like upgrading your home. Your most important job is to become intimately familiar with the numbers that exist in your life and the numbers for what you're trying to do.

"Nail down your cost of living in a very honest way." Behr suggested. "Get serious about tracking your cash flow, not because you need to be on a tight budget or you're in debt or anything, but to be honest about how much you spend and how much you want to spend."

Without honesty, around everything, you can't be sure you're hedging enough.

Four months after our interview, I learned that Tamara took a new job.

"When we spoke, I had no idea I would end up back," she told me. "But when I saw an opportunity along with a gap in our trajectory, I thought, let me help in this way and bring in money."

She explained, the financials provided by the prior owners didn't really match up with what they were experiencing. They thought they could maintain their existing lifestyle with what the practice would earn off the bat, but maybe didn't account for the costs of all those changes. The money pinch didn't feel good.

"One of the only arguments that we would ever get into was around finances," she said. "It was the first time in our relationship that we had to be so careful about everything."

She also learned that she wasn't passionate about the day-to-day responsibilities of what her role ended up being. "I don't want to be a biller or the head of the office," she realized. Besides, most of the sweeping changes she implemented were already in action, and that critical need for her skillset no longer amounted to a full-time job. She still runs all the marketing on the side, but she's happy to have her own thing going again.

"I was missing a big chunk of my separate life," she admitted.

You learn a lot about yourself taking big risks, too.

"When I was interviewing again, I told them, I've contributed what I need to contribute. Now it's his job to run with it, and I need to bring in money so I can invest back into his business. We need to buy the building. We need to buy new equipment. We need to invest in the facelift of the company. My money can help us do so."

Tamara is quick—she figured it out. She gave Andy the tools to get started, but the next best thing she could give him was a hedge.

29.
A MILLION WAYS HOME

Being prepared is better than trying to predict what will happen.

Dating back to the millennial aughts, I've spent most of my career working in the Financial District in New York City. My first job was at a law firm on Maiden Lane, where the long shadow of 9/11 loomed in the absence of the buildings and people who were gone.

My late boss remembered everything about Orientation Day nine years before I sat with him around the same conference table a few blocks from the hole left in the ground: the planes, the confusion, the fear, the choices. He didn't wait for anyone to tell him what to do. He got his people out as fast as he could. I had a sneaking suspicion he told us that story because he wanted us to know he'd do it again.

Preparing for the next terrorist attack was a cornerstone of corporate safety when you worked downtown in the decade-plus after. We'd cram into the elevator banks and listen to the fire marshal's protocols while our team safety leads pointed to our assigned stairwells to use when our floor was called.

I always thought of Dan, having his own plan.

Because of him, Douglas and I created an ICE Plan—that's, In Case of Emergency—to map out what we would do if a crisis occurred. We accounted for scenarios where we could meet up and where we couldn't. We had exit routes from the city. We had emergency contacts. We had (we still have) each other saved in our phones as "ICE."

We didn't plan because we were afraid of another terrorist attack. (As a testament to that, our current office sits high atop one of the World Trade Center buildings, which I am proud to have watched rise from the ruins.) We made plans to prepare for *anything*—the thinkable and the unthinkable. Thankfully, we've never had to find out if our plans work. But, I do know that we have a better shot than anyone who has never thought it through.

In his second book, *Same As Ever*, Morgan Housel wrote about risk being what you don't see. He wrote, you can't plan for what you can't imagine. The more you're convinced you've thought of everything, the more shocked you'll be when something else occurs. None of us is Nostradamus, which is why it's more important to prepare than predict.[59]

I spoke to Housel about outcomes. Most people prefer to ignore the bad ones altogether.

"A big thing is the idea that it can't happen to you," he said. "It's easy to gawk at people who've been diagnosed with a serious medical illness, gotten divorced, or lost their job and think, *wow, sucks for them*, without realizing that it can happen to you, too."

The odds of us experiencing at least some of these bad things in our lifetime is almost certain. We lose jobs. We get sick. We all die (womp, I'm sorry). Lots of bad outcomes are out of our control, and that thought scares many away from acknowledging the truth.

In writing this book, I've thought a lot about my own fears. I was

29. A MILLION WAYS HOME

so afraid of losing a parent, but I never imagined my dad would brush death, which would set forth a chain of events impacting the rest of my childhood, which would bleed into my career decisions, my financial choices, and my adult relationship with my husband. And yet, everyone loses their parents. One spouse will lay the other to rest. We just don't know when, so we hope for never.

Housel and I agree that people underestimate the potential for bad outcomes, because they are trying to self-preserve. Emotionally, it's much easier to default back on your optimism bias that it will *all just work out* than to acknowledge the range of possibilities, good and bad. When it comes to money, couples are afraid to plan, because they have to say the hard parts out loud:

> *We are afraid to admit our pasts are still present.*
> *We are afraid to work through shame.*
> *We are afraid to admit we don't know certain things.*
> *We are afraid to acknowledge our goals have changed.*
> *We are afraid of not knowing what comes next.*

The problem with living a reactive life is losing the opportunity to plan for the good stuff, too. The tools you need to prepare for one are the same tools you need to plan for the other: numbers, hedges, honesty, and flexibility. Just as Douglas and I prepared those different routes to take in the event of an emergency, we began to thrive and move towards our goals when we embraced that there are so many ways to get there—not just the ways everyone else takes, but the ways that feel most authentic to us.

"You kind of get fooled into thinking that life is a straight line, especially through a lot of the guidance and content that's out there around financial planning," said Taylor Schulte, CFP®. "You believe if you just do this and this, you'll get from here to here, but it just doesn't work that way."

Schulte explained how he helps couples stress-test their finances for anything that can happen.

"Sometimes clients feel like there's only one or two options: *I either do this or I do that*. And we'll challenge them to come up with ten solutions. Once they come up with those ten solutions, come up with ten more," he said. "We sometimes feel very limited by our options, and all of a sudden, you start to get creative and force yourself to come up with these different ideas and you really surprise yourselves."

To illustrate, if you're saving for a home and one of you loses your job, that doesn't mean you can't keep trying to buy a new home. Maybe you take on some freelance projects with a part-time job, or maybe you look for that home in a lower cost-of-living town, or maybe you downsize your current living space to continue saving at the pace you are saving. I'm not suggesting one of these options is better than the other—just that options exist, if you want to keep going. You don't need to just throw in the towel.

"It's not this or that, right? It's not one or the other. Everything is possible," he said.

When you accept that a million outcomes have a million paths to get there, you can be easier on each other when the path changes. You will have the emotional flexibility to support each other, because you've prepared for what will happen when you don't know what will happen. Being nimble means being easier on each other. It values the journey as much as the end.

30. THE GREATEST RISK IS DOING NOTHING

We all leave a mark on the people we love. The question is, what mark do you want to leave?

Well, you've reached the end. We're sorry if you were waiting for budgeting tips. Thankfully, there's tons of books on those.

Early in the process of interviewing couples, we stopped asking too much about the numbers. Many still told us, of course, but we didn't want to focus on how much money people made. It's a relevant question with respect to your partner, but with respect to the rest of the world, who cares? The challenges that test relationships in this book can look the same inside a penthouse or a mobile home. They are relative. They are personal. They get resolved *within* the relationship—not on a tax return.

What mattered more was how couples felt about what they had.

We wanted to know how money made them feel. What motivated them. What worried them. What upset them. What felt fair. What they overcame to get to this place. What they yearned for, and how they planned to get there.

We asked whether they had *enough*—and we ask you the same—because a truthful answer to this question reveals what's most important in your life. Again, tax brackets had little to do with how couples replied. They have *enough* because they have their health. They have faith. They have family. They have love, or have loved, here in this lifetime.

Most who think they don't quite have *enough* aren't trying to gain entry to Billionaires' Row. They have tangible hopes and achievable goals. They just want to do a little better than their parents did. They want to offer lessons—not handouts—and create more opportunities for their kids. They want to chase experiences that create stories to pass from generation to generation. In the least egotistical way possible, people just don't want to be forgotten. Greater than any gift they could give, they want their values to outlive them.

I've thought a lot about legacy in doing this work.

My dad's dad told me all that matters is my blood and my money, but he died before knowing who I'd be. I chased what I thought mattered in the shadow of his last words, but none of it made me happier. None of it helped my relationship with Douglas. All the while, my mom's parents stood by my side through everything. Married more than 65 years, they were the pillars of stability in my life. Despite their modest means, every bite my Pop-Pop ate, every show he saw, every song he heard, was the "greatest of his life." He was just happy to be around his friends, his family, his only grandchild. I carry a fuller heart knowing I was part of their *enough*.

The legacy they left me is how to love without conditions. I've realized, giving this to my husband and daughters is what matters most to me, too.

30. THE GREATEST RISK IS DOING NOTHING

Love—not money—builds the legacy you want.

We all leave a lasting impact on the people closest to us. The question is, what kind of impact do you want to leave?

If you've made it here, you care about where you and your partner stand with money. You should want to be standing side-by-side, but that doesn't mean you are at this very moment. One of you could be in front, or behind, or invisible. This could be your fault, or theirs, or no one's in particular. But you will only know by communicating. When you turn away from the dynamics playing out in your relationship, you perpetuate the greatest risk of all: not finding out.

Money isn't a team game you win once. You have to play it forever.

Navigating the themes we've explored in this book is a practice—not a solution. You should always be trying to:

explore where you're from;
move on from your mistakes;
honor each other's contributions;
identify the powers that serve you and don't;
and approach uncertainty as a team.

Your work cannot end lest you wish to lose your footing when the next challenge comes to test you, and it will. It always does. That's just life.

If you have even a sliver of your time on this earth to be more curious about someone you love, you need to take it. You will wish you took it.

Just as I wanted better for us, I want better for you.

You deserve a love better than riches, and you can achieve it together.

YOUR QUESTIONS ON RISK

1. Are you willing to spend money for a chance to make more money?
2. What's worse: losing money or missing out?
3. How do you feel about what you can't control?
4. Where do you carry the most risk: your career, your portfolio, your health, or your reputation?
5. How are you hedging that risk?
6. Think of your next major life goal together. When do you want it to happen?
7. Explore five different paths to that goal. Are there behaviors or circumstances you need to change to get there?
8. What are your non-negotiables to feeling safe and cared for?
9. You win a million dollars (after taxes). What do you do with it?
10. What is the most important thing you will leave behind?

RESOURCE REMINDER

As mentioned at the start of this book, you can scan the QR code below to quickly access all of the questions we included throughout, so that you can take them anywhere you go.

ACKNOWLEDGMENTS

We began with you—and a lot about me.

Douglas and I knew that my money story was unique. As we spent many hours with couples and experts over the course of two years, truth poured out of me in ways I could never have expected. Still, this book was never meant to be a memoir so much as love stories with money as a main character in them. We left a lot of our personal lives on the cutting room floor, and the stories we did share were targeted, edited, and based on our own recollections and points of view. There wasn't space to write about the love and care my parents showed me even as they went their separate ways. About the reconciliations and forgiveness and healing between us. About the Thanksgivings we can now spend around one dinner table. There wasn't a place to draw this full circle for you, so I am doing it here. I want to thank my parents, Robin and Ed, for loving me enough to recognize the personal significance this work carries in my life and supporting me through it, even if it's hard for all of us. And to Melissa, you are a piece of our pie, too.

As for our daughters, they rock our world. They are perfect, in the sense that they are imperfectly who they are, and having the opportunity to raise them is our true definition of wealth. Even our most difficult times as a young family during the pandemic

ACKNOWLEDGMENTS

were draped with the duality of joy on top. That's parenthood for you. Hazel and Ruby, you are loved beyond riches. You are enough.

We would like to thank our friends and colleagues who stepped up for us. These include men and women in the financial services industry who embraced me following my dramatic career pivot and continue to say our names in rooms we're not in. They also include our closest friends with whom we can laugh after a long week, cry over how big our kids are getting, and truly just be happy for each other. And of course, our Internet Friends, as I used to call everyone who Douglas ever befriended on the platform formerly known as Twitter. I once believed you couldn't make real friends online. Now, some of my favorite relationships began on a screen, including with some of the Internet Fairy Godmothers who got me through writing this book. You don't need to be present to have a presence. Our village is wherever we choose.

We also need to acknowledge the couples we interviewed. When we asked, "Would you be willing to talk about money and your relationship?" they said, "Sure!" Well, some of them said sure. Others joined our Zoom room having no idea what their spouses signed them up for, and yet—amazingly—they also showed up. For every single person who showed up: allow us to express our heartfelt gratitude for your time, candor, and willingness to go there. You let us into some of the most complex, uncomfortable parts of your lives. Your stories weighed heavy on us, and I hope we did them justice. It's wild to think how much has changed in your lives since we first started speaking with you, but I guess that's the point. Life is fluid. Things change. We are all in constant motion. Thank you for letting us onto your ride, even if just to paint a picture from one moment in time. You've changed our lives more than you know. All of your stories matter.

You should know, we have different *whys* for writing this book.

Through his work, Douglas meets people who know a lot about money and people who don't. Knowledge gaps in financial literacy often exist where systemic challenges lie, and he wants to do everything he can do to fill those gaps. When you start seeing the real consequences of when spouses can't come together on a function as critical to their relationship as money, it humbles you. Missed meetings lead to missed opportunities lead to unwelcome surprises and much worse. A few years back, we attended a founder's summit and heard from an executive at one of the world's largest banks. He shared with the audience that they don't usually get to speak with most of their high-net-worth female clients until their spouses die. I almost didn't believe it, but Douglas did. He's sat across those tables, and he knows that ending up there isn't something that happens in a day. That's why educating anyone who's been disengaged from their finances will not happen in a day, either. It takes time, and practice, and patience. It takes love and understanding. He wants this book to help you find your way on the path that makes sense for you.

He also just wants people to be happy. I think he'd like to save a marriage or two. That's the fixer in him who never gives up.

I'm all about equity. Claudia Goldin, who won the Nobel Prize in economics for her studies of women's progress in the workforce, said: "We're never going to have gender equality until we also have couple equity." I believe every word of this deep in my soul. Spreading the household responsibilities with greater care has a direct impact on how women advance their careers, and thus, narrows the gender pay gap on a societal level. But beyond improving our workplace representation, women deserve greater visibility for *all* their work. Caregivers deserve to be treated as the providers that they are, and income shouldn't dictate the way couples value each other's time.

I want every woman to know that when financial decisions get made, you deserve a seat at that table. You deserve to be heard. You deserve for your opinions to matter. Like an investment portfolio, equity in your relationship requires a constant search

ACKNOWLEDGMENTS

for balance. I wanted to show you what that can look like. I wanted to help you find it.

So, just like you and your partner might have different *whys* behind your money, we have different *whys* for writing this book. And still, our shared perspective got us here. Imagine where yours can take you.

ABOUT THE AUTHORS

Douglas Boneparth, CFP®, is the founder of Bone Fide Wealth, a wealth management firm in New York City. Recognized as one of the nation's most influential financial advisors, Douglas serves on the advisory councils for *CNBC* and *Investopedia*. He has been featured in *The New York Times*, *The Wall Street Journal*, *Barron's*, and more. He is also a CFP Board Ambassador for New York. Douglas received his B.S. from the University of Florida and his MBA from NYU's Stern School of Business. When he's not making jokes on the internet, he enjoys brewing coffee, though he can do both at the same time.

Heather Boneparth is used to wearing many hats. On her first maternity leave, she co-authored the couple's first book on helping millennials achieve financial freedom. Since then, she has become a rising voice at the intersection of love, money, and family. She has written for *CNBC*, *theSkimm*, *Insider*, and more. As a lawyer, she spent more than a decade in the insurance industry before joining the family business as Bone Fide Wealth's director of business and legal affairs. She received her B.S. from the University of Florida and her J.D. from the Benjamin N. Cardozo School of Law.

Heather and Douglas met in college and consider themselves Gators for life. They now live in New Jersey with their two daughters. For more, subscribe to *The Joint Account*, their newsletter helping couples talk about money.

ENDNOTES

1   "Relationship Intimacy Being Crushed by Financial Tension: AICPA Survey," *The American Institute of CPAs (AICPA)* (February 4, 2021), www.businesswire.com.

2   Chase Peterson-Withorn, "For Richer or Richest: Inside the Billion-Dollar Marriages, Open Relationships and Bitter Divorces of the Forbes 400," *Forbes* (May 9, 2021), www.forbes.com.

3   Lauren M. Papp, Ph.D., E. Mark Cummings, Ph.D., and Marcie C. Goeke-Morey, Ph.D., "Richer, for Poorer: Money as a Topic of Marital Conflict in the Home," *Family Relations: An Interdisciplinary Journal of Applied Family Studies*, 58, no. 1 (2009).

4   Oksana Yakushko and Charles Eckhart, "Sustaining Relational Capital: Contributions from Attachment Theory to Financial Advising and Wealth Management," *Journal of Wealth Management* 26, no. 4 (2024).

5   Kristen Wong, "How Your Childhood Memories Affect Your Adult Relationship With Money," *Well + Good* (November 1, 2017), www.wellandgood.com.

6   Luigi Guiso, Paola Sapienza, and Luigi Zingales, "Does Culture Affect Economic Outcomes?" *Journal of Economic Perspectives*, 20, no. 2 (2006).

7   Gillian Tett, "How Culture Shapes Our Money Mentality," *Financial Times* (June 18, 2021), www.ft.com.

8   Kristen Broady, Mac McComas, and Amine Ouazad, "An Analysis of Financial Institutions in Black-majority Communities: Black Borrowers and Depositors Face Considerable Challenges Accessing Banking Services," *The Brookings Institution* (November 2, 2021), www.brookings.edu/articles.

9   "2023 FDIC National Survey of Unbanked and Underbanked Households–Executive Summary," *FDIC* (July 24, 2023), www.fdic.gov/household-survey.

10 Oyin Adedoyin and Sanaa Rowser, "Black Investors are the Biggest New Group of Stock Buyers," *The Wall Street Journal* (January 15, 2024), www.wsj.com.

11 Joe Pinsker, "Why So Many Americans Don't Talk About Money," *The Atlantic* (March 2, 2020), www.theatlantic.com.

12   *See* David Robson, "How East and West Think in Profoundly Different Ways," *BBC* (January 19, 2017), www.bbc.com.

13   Daniel Crosby, *The Soul of Wealth: 50 Reflections on Money and Meaning*, (Harriman House, 2024).

14   Ashley LeBaron-Black, et al., "Finances, Religion, and the FAAR Model: How Religion Exacerbates and Alleviates Financial Stress," American Psychological Association, *Psychology of Religion and Spirituality* 13, no. 3 (2019).

15   Figures as of 2020. Jennifer Wirth, "ADHD Statistics and Facts," *Forbes* (August 24, 2023), www.forbes.com.

16   Tiffany Curtis, "How Being Neurodiverse Affects Your Relationship With Money," *NerdWallet* (March 16, 2023), www.nerdwallet.com.

17   Liz Moor and Sam Friedman, "Justifying Inherited Wealth: Between the 'Bank of Mum and Dad' and the Meritocratic Ideal," *Economy and Society*, 50, no. 4 (2021).

18   Laura Feiveson and John Sabelhaus, "How Does Intergenerational Wealth Transmission Affect Wealth Concentration?" FEDS Notes, Washington: Board of Governors of the Federal Reserve System (June 1, 2018).

19   "More Couples are Signing Prenups Before Saying 'I Do'," *The Harris Poll* (July 12, 2022), www.theharrispoll.com.

20   Eric Reed, "Average American Inheritance, By Wealth Level," *Yahoo! Finance* (March 23, 2024), www.finance.yahoo.com.

21   Doug Luftman, "Community Property States & Definition," Trust & Will, www.trustandwill.com. Time for a disclaimer: this is not legal advice, and what is deemed "individual property" or "community property" depends on your state of residence and individual circumstances, which should be discussed with a lawyer.

22   "About Adverse Childhood Experiences." *Centers for Disease Control and Prevention* (October 8, 2024), www.cdc.gov/aces/about.

23   Cynthia L. Harter and John F.R. Harter, "The Link Between Adverse Childhood Experiences and Financial Security in Adulthood," *Journal of Family and Economic Issues*, 43, no. 4 (2022).

24   Jenny Olson, Scott Rick, et al., "Common Cents: Bank Account Structure and Couples' Relationship Dynamics," *Journal of Consumer Research*, 50, no. 4 (2023).

25   Melanie Hanson, "Student Loan Debt Statistics," EducationData.org, last updated March 16, 2025, www.educationdata.org/student-loan-debt-statistics.

26   Sarah Foster, "As Student Loan Payments Resume, Financial Regrets and Stress Grip Borrowers," *Bankrate* (September 25, 2023), www.bankrate.com.

27   *See, e.g.*, Brené Brown, "Listening to shame," TED Conference, Long Beach, California (March 16, 2012), excerpt available on YouTube.

28   Beverly Harzog, "Survey: Nearly 45% Had Credit Card Debt Before Paying for a Wedding," *U.S. News & World Report* (February 15, 2023), www.money.usnews.com.

29   Anna Tranfaglia, Alicia Lloro and Ellen Merry, "Question Design and the Gender Gap in Financial Literacy," FEDS Notes, Washington: Board of Governors of the Federal Reserve System (January 02, 2024).

ENDNOTES

30   "Cult," *Merriam-Webster.com Dictionary*, accessed July 1, 2024.

31   Peter Gratton, "What is MLM? How Multilevel Marketing Works," *Investopedia*, updated March 28, 2025, www.investopedia.com.

32   We will spare you the text of the actual court decision, though it is linked in the references to the article. Here's a brief summary of In re Amway Corp.(1979), *Wikipedia.org.*, accessed April 2, 2025, www.en.wikipedia.org.

33   "Direct Selling Market Size, Share, Growth, Trends, Statistics Analysis Report, By Direct Selling Types (Single Level Direct Selling, Party Plan, Multi-Level Marketing, Online Shopping and Venue Sales), By Product Type (Fashion and Apparel, Health and Wellness, Cosmetics and Personal Care, and Others), by Region, and Segment Forecasts, 2025-2033," DataHorizzon Research, accessed April 2, 2025, www.datahorizzonresearch.com.

34   "Direct Selling in the United States 2022 Industry Overview," Direct Selling Association, www.dsa.org.

35   Katie Kelton, "Survey: Two in Five Americans in a Relationship Have Kept a Financial Secret from Their Partner," *Bankrate* (January 27, 2025), www.bankrate.com.

36   "Relationship Intimacy Being Crushed by Financial Tension: AICPA Survey," *The American Institute of CPAs (AICPA)* (February 4, 2021), www.businesswire.com.

37   Jenny Olson, Emily Garbinsky, *et al.*, "Love, Lies and Money: Financial Infidelity in Romantic Relationships," *Journal of Consumer Research*, 47, no. 1 (2020).

38   "What is Perinatal Depression?" American Psychiatric Association (October, 2023), www.psychiatry.org.

39   Kiley Hurst, "U.S. Women are Outpacing Men in College Completion, Including in Every Major Racial and Ethnic Group," Pew Research Center (November 18, 2024), www.pewresearch.org.

40   Richard Fry, "Women Now Outnumber Men in the U.S. College-Educated Labor Force," Pew Research Center (September 26, 2022), www.pewresearch.org.

41   LeanIn.Org and McKinsey & Company, "Women in the Workplace: The 10th Anniversary Report," 2024, www.leanin.org/women-in-the-workplace.

42   Molly Weston Williamson, "The State of Paid Family and Medical Leave in the U.S. in 2024," The Center for American Progress (January 17, 2024), www.americanprogress.org.

43   Care.com, "This is How Much Childcare Costs in 2025" (January 29, 2025), www.care.com.

44   Shengwei Sun, "Women and Families Struggle with Child Care Following the Federal Funding Cliff, But Care Better in States with Additional State Funding for Child Care," National Women's Law Center (May 3, 2024), www.nwlc.org.

45   Richard Fry, *et al.*, "In a Growing Share of U.S. Marriages, Husbands and Wives Earn About the Same," Pew Research Center (April 13, 2023), www.pewresearch.org.

46   Bruce Horovitz, "New AARP Report Finds Family Caregivers Provide $600 Billion in Unpaid Care Across the U.S.," *AARP* (March 8, 2023), www.aarp.org.